Death,
A
New
Beginning

Sarah LaNelle Menet

Death, A New Beginning

Previous Publishing Information

Contents

Preface

I wish to share some important messages with you as you read this book. I have experienced many difficulties and tragedies that I will tell you about. You will read about serious future events that could affect your life. All that we experience in this life, good and bad, helps us grow and is part of God's great plan for us. I personally want you to know that I know that God lives and He is our father. He knows each of us by name and loves us more than we can comprehend.

Jesus Christ is the Savior and Redeemer of this world, and our shield and our buckler. If we give our full trust to and keep faith in our Savior and our father, no matter what comes, all will be well with us. Be at peace, fear not. Put on the armor of complete faith. It will all be worth it. I truly love and care about all of you.

With great love,
Sarah Menet

Acknowledgments

I sincerely want to express my love and appreciation to my Heavenly Father and His Son Jesus Christ for the trials and triumphs I have experienced thus far in this journey we call life.

I am grateful to have been given an understanding of how we lived before we came to earth, why we are here and the meaning of life, and what waits for us when we leave this existence.

I am thankful for all of the people who spent so much time helping put this book together. It took many hours to transcribe the telling of my experience. The first version of the book was completed in a little over two weeks, which was not enough time to share all that I wanted to share. I think I could talk for 24 hours a day for 20 years and not be able to share everything I learned on the other side.

Among those who have made the production of this book possible, special appreciation is extended to Nick Mills for his continual, amazing efforts to edit and prepare this book for publication. And without the months of typing by John Mount it may not have ever emerged to where Nick could work on it. Roger Young and Allan South laid the groundwork to publish this material and Allan continues the process. To all who have helped, thank you.

I pray that God our father will bless me with the inspiration and health to be able to help bring more of my brothers and sisters to the knowledge and understanding of where they came from and why they are here. Truly, every living being is a literal son or daughter of deity, and He loves us more than we'll ever understand in this life.

Introduction

There is nothing new about near-death experiences (NDEs). They have been happening since history began. Sarah's experience is of great interest for several reasons, among which are the extensive detail and unusual scope of her visit to the world beyond and the way it relates to her life's story. She describes in detail what she saw in the spirit world, the food, the people, the buildings, the animals, the colors and so many amazingly interesting things. She not only visited a world of light, but also was taken to visit a place of extreme darkness and pain.

She has emerged from her NDE and her incredibly difficult life as a strong and fervent voice for good conduct and a more noble and kind view of each other in our mortal experience.

Her ability to influence minds and hearts toward a more enlightened and hopeful outlook has been life-changing to many distressed souls as well as to many who are searching for answers. If this book does no more than show that someone can go through all the trials that Sarah has gone through and emerge victorious, it would be completely worth all efforts to write and publish this book. But there is much more here, including warnings of impending difficulties.

Many people ask two questions concerning this book: When did she start telling people about her experience, including the events she saw in the future, and what religion or church did she belong to when she had the experience?

Sarah had her death experience in 1979 and for many years told only a few people about it. Then in 1988, when she almost died a second time, she felt strongly that she needed to tell more people of her experience, including what she saw happening in the future.

Sarah is on video tape as early as 1995 talking about tall buildings in New York falling down, an economic collapse in the United States and around the world, a devastating biological attack on the United States, a global war and other events.

At the time Sarah had her experience, she was not a member of any organized religion. In fact, though raised a Christian, she had become agnostic, believing that there was probably not a God. She therefore didn't care about religious questions or concerns.

It should be noted that even after her experience her life has not been easy. In 1996, she suddenly became blind because of her diabetes and a few days later collapsed from kidney failure and congestive heart failure. When she left the hospital, the doctors told her she needed to begin dialysis immediately or she would probably die within a few months because her kidneys were only functioning at approximately one percent.

She refused, however, and, unbelievably, continues to function at a high level. She talks about her experience to those who will listen. She has spent a lot of time in the hospice program and counsels often with those who have gone through or are going through tremendous trials of their own. She offers hope, compassion and insight as she uniquely can. She keeps saying time is running out for our society faster than is commonly understood.

Sarah says she looks forward to the time when she will be called back to the world of spirits she visited and be in the presence of her Savior one more time because she knows that there really is no such thing as death. It is only a new beginning for the next phase of our eternal existence.

CHAPTER 1

My Life Before

When a person leaves their physical body, we call it "Death." However, a person never really dies. The physical body is laid in the earth, but the person's spirit returns to God and lives forever. When a person dies from an illness or an accident, those on the other side refer to this transition as the "New Birth."

When I made the decision to take my life, I had hoped for complete oblivion and the elimination of all memory of my mortal life. I had believed that there was no God, and therefore no afterlife. When I suddenly found myself watching from somewhere near the ceiling, as the police and paramedics worked on my body, I learned that I had been quite wrong.

I need to share some of the events of my early years to help the reader understand the choices that I made later on in my life. This is not a "pity me" story, even though I was depressed for many years.

When I was five, our family obtained a small black and white television. I never watched regular children's programs like cartoons, etc., but I was fascinated with and loved Westerns. One of my first of many favorites was the series "Rin Tin Tin." I fell in love with this amazing

German Shepherd and vowed that someday I would have one just like him.

At this same age, I watched "Roy Rogers and Dale Evans." Then, at the age of nine, I watched a program called "The Rifleman." It was about a father raising his boy alone. The young actor Johnny Crawford starred as his son, Mark McCain, in this series. I thought he was the most beautiful thing I had ever seen. When I was nine years old, I remember telling my mother that when I grew up, I was going to marry him. She looked at me with a gentle smile, but sarcastically said, "Of course, LaNelle." Years later, I met Johnny Crawford in Kanab, Utah, where many of the famous western stars gathered every summer to entertain visitors and sign photographs. I was also able to meet Johnny's beautiful wife, Charlotte. We three became good friends.

Sarah (LaNelle) with Johnny Crawford

11

I looked forward to watching all of the Westerns such as "Wyatt Earp," "Gunsmoke," "Rawhide," "Bonanza," and my favorite, "The Big Valley." I often wished that I had lived in that time period. Their lives seemed to have more simplicity, even though they had to work hard. I loved the antique furniture in the houses and the style of clothing that the women wore.

I played with a girl down the street named Linda Adams. Her mother, Mary Jane Adams, was my mother's best friend. She baked homemade bread nearly every day that I was there. We ate a lot of the dough while she formed the bread into the baking pans. While it was baking, the house smelled wonderful. Each time I make homemade bread, it brings back that wonderful memory.

LaNelle and Linda

I loved horses, dogs, cats, birds, and even more unusual pets that little girls normally wouldn't like. I played with frogs, lizards, and small garden snakes. Most of all, I loved turtles.

One afternoon, while playing in the neighborhood and climbing fences, I saw a large turtle in a neighbor's back yard. I wanted it more than anything. I returned home and told my mother that I was going to go on a turtle hunt. She laughed and said, "OK, well good luck." She was accustomed to my out of the ordinary activities.

I went back and took the turtle out of the neighbor's backyard. When I arrived home with the turtle, my mother figured out exactly what had happened. She was upset that I had done something dishonest.

I ran and hid my "new pet" in the front room closet and covered it with blankets. After receiving a good lecture, I retrieved the turtle and took it back to its rightful owner. It was my first lesson not to take something that belonged to someone else. To my embarrassment, my sisters still repeat this story every chance they get.

Tim M.

The book called "A Tale of Two Cities" begins with the sentence, "It was the best of times, it was the worst of times." For me, it was a time of great happiness and hope for a bright future, yet it was also a time of devastating tragedy.

In the early 1960's, while attending Simi Valley High School, I met a very special and unusual young man. His name was Tim M., a person to me not only handsome and popular, but loved by everyone who knew him at school. He was romantic, kind, sensitive, and very much a gentleman. Over several weeks of spending a lot of time together, we eventually became boyfriend and girlfriend.

On our first real date, he took me to a movie. Part way through the film, a particular scene appeared and he suddenly stood up and said, "We're leaving." I realized he was protecting me from seeing an inappropriate scene. It made me care even more for him. After our date, when he walked me to the door, he asked me if he could kiss me good night. I had just turned 16 years old and had never experienced this with anyone before. The kiss was brief, sweet, and respectful.

As summer approached, Tim planned to go to Oregon with his parents to support their dream of building a log cabin for their retirement. My mother was afraid that Tim and I were getting too close and insisted that I go with her to Salt Lake City for the summer. She promised we would return in September when it was time for school to start again. Being separated from Tim for three months felt more like a hundred years to me. We promised to write to each other every day and describe everything we had accomplished.

We wrote letters back and forth for approximately one month. My mother routinely mailed my letters to him on her way to work and I anxiously waited for the postman to arrive and deliver any letters Tim had written to me.

One day, my mother told me that we were leaving Salt Lake City, and moving to Sandy, Utah, where I would be attending yet another high school. I had a difficult time adjusting to another new situation. I wondered why we were moving to Sandy when we were supposed to be returning to California very soon.

I was obviously upset about the whole arrangement and to make matters even worse, I suddenly stopped receiving letters from Tim. I wondered if he had met another girl in Oregon, or maybe his feelings for me were just a passing teenage crush and now it was over.

I basically stopped eating and cried often. My mother became very worried about my behavior and promised we would return to California in December. We would be home for Christmas. I could hardly wait to find out what had happened with this special relationship Tim and I shared.

He taught me so many things about the world and most of all about the moon and the stars, and he helped me understand and recognize the constellations. When together, we often spent time gazing at the diamonds in the sky. One of our favorite pastimes was to bake chocolate chip cookies together nearly every week. I loved playing the guitar and singing for him. His favorite hobby was photography and everywhere we went, he took pictures of me. It drove me crazy but in a funny and precious way.

One day after I returned home from school, I saw a letter on the table for me from a girlfriend named Shelly Kinkade who attended Simi High School. She told me that on October 31, Halloween night, Tim was riding in a car with his best friend Bruce. Bruce was driving way too fast down Sinaloa Boulevard. He was going so fast that his car could not negotiate the sharp curve. The car tipped over, throwing Tim out, dragging and crushing his body until the car came to a complete stop.

By the time I received Shelly's letter, Tim had already been buried in the Simi Valley Cemetery. Shelly said that nearly every student had put his or her high school ring into the casket. This signified to me how much everyone loved him.

Not long after that, I discovered that my mother had not been mailing my letters to Tim and had been throwing his letters to me away. When we returned to Simi Valley, I could not bear to attend school or to do anything with friends. I only left the house to walk to the cemetery every day and sit by his grave. Sometimes I would be there for four or five hours talking to him, leaning against his headstone and crying.

Returning home from one of these visits, my mother expressed how concerned she was about the depression I was feeling. She asked me to come into the room where a clergyman stood waiting to talk with me. They both wanted to know if I was so devastated because I had been physically involved with Tim. I became hysterical and screamed at both of them. They did not know what a sweet and good boy he was nor did they know that I was sweet and good too. How dare they sully the beautiful memories I had of him.

15

Within a few weeks, I went to visit Tim's parents. His mother took me into his room. They never packed his belongings away. They had left it just as it was the night that he died. Dozens of pictures that Tim had taken of me were hung up all over the walls. His mother walked over to his dresser and opened a drawer. She then handed me all the letters that I had sent to him. I couldn't help but break out in tears, thinking that they meant so much to him that he kept every one of them. All the time when I was thinking he met someone else, he could have been thinking the same thing about me.

After this, I could not stay with my mother, or in Simi Valley any more. I returned to Joanne's foster home for my last year of School at Venice High.

In reference now to some of the "best" of times, despite the fact that Joanne's mother was pretty intolerant of my living there, I truly loved attending Venice High and enjoyed Joanne's friendship and company. We did a lot of fun things together and were truly best friends. I always introduced her as my sister.

History was one of my favorite classes. I was approximately seventeen years old and my teacher Steve was thirty-two. He frequently called me to the front of the classroom and handed me his keys to go out into the parking lot and retrieve items he needed from his car. My fellow students began whispering and making jokes about how often he would ask me to do errands for him. Rumors started flying. Running errands for my teacher did feel a little strange the first time he asked me. He told me his car was the butterscotch Porsche. I had no idea what a Porsche looked like and spent about 20 minutes going through the parking lot trying to find that particular color and model of car.

Every time I attended football games he stood or sat next to me on the bleachers. At dances, he would make comments like, "I wish I could ask you to dance." In the beginning, I liked and was flattered by his attention, until one evening in his car he kissed me. It was too aggressive and I did not like it. I got out of his car on Venice Boulevard, late at night, and started walking home. A car full of boys pulled over and ordered me to get into their car. Instead, I ran to a neighboring house, followed closely by one of the boys. I was scared. I banged on the door but no one answered. I ran to the next house, and just opened the door and rushed in. I slammed the door, frightening the elderly couple inside. The husband said, "It's too dangerous to walk home in this neighborhood," so he offered to take me home.

My foster sister Joanne and I found my history teacher's address in Manhattan Beach and drove to his apartment. I had hoped to talk with him about what had happened in his car. We knocked on the door and his wife answered and invited us in. What a bizarre and awkward moment that was! He never wore his wedding ring at school and judging by the way he treated me in front of the other students, I would never have thought that he was married.

Joanne

This ended his little crush on me. I refused to take the final and dropped out of his history class. I began to discover something about myself. I came to the realization that I didn't like boys or men that were pushy or too aggressive. I preferred guys with more of a quiet and refined personality.

Meanwhile, a lot of other changes in my life took place. I moved into another foster home with the Clifford family. I had been chosen to play the lead role of Maria in the musical "The

Sound of Music." Then, with only four months left until I would have graduated, my parents pulled me out of the present home and made me return to Simi Valley. I was disappointed that I lost the opportunity to be in the musical.

I loved entertaining and performing. I continued entering talent shows and musical competitions. I had been doing that since the age of twelve when I bought my first guitar. I had taught myself how to play and entered talent shows throughout the Los Angeles area. I won first place several times with songs I had composed myself. Most of those songs were written for the young actor on "The Rifleman" previously mentioned. I'd had a crush on him since I was nine years old.

During this time, I recorded a 45 RPM record at Ledbetter's in Westwood with two of my songs. A Los Angeles DJ wanted to promote some of my music on his radio program. Once again, my parents put a stop to this. They were afraid I would get mixed up in the entertainment business, which has destroyed so many young people.

Sarah (LaNelle), Age 15, Talent Show

But these were the bright spots in my childhood. However, it is necessary to talk about the dark times in my early years to understand the dramatic change that came into my heart because of my near-death experience, and why it happened.

A Living Hell

It was horrible growing up in Los Angeles as a child. My existence seemed like a bad dream. Every day was a nightmare, and it continue to get worse as I grew older.

There was always tension in the house. On one day, my parents were having a terrible argument. My father was screaming at my mother as he yelled, cursed, and threw things. I was always terrified of my father and couldn't bear to be around him. Their fighting unsettled me, so I went outside and climbed into our car because I didn't want to hear them arguing. I eventually fell asleep in the back seat. Apparently, they had been looking all over the neighborhood for me. When they found me, I received a sound whipping because my father was so angry.

He would get angry at the drop of a hat. Punishments were a regular part of life in our home. These were not spankings, they were whippings, often with objects. On a few occasions, he would hit us with a police weapon called a "blackjack," a thick leather strap with steel balls in the ends. His temper could flare up for any reason.

At the age of eight, my parents were once again separated, as they had been several times before. I stayed home sick from school and was sleeping on my mother's bed. I woke up hearing a struggle in our apartment. As I entered the living room, I saw my father choking my mother to death. When he saw me, he dropped my mother to the floor. I believe he would have killed her had he not seen me. I called my mother's best friend, Mary Jane Adams. When this happened, I went to stay with

Father & Mother,
Linda, Deborah, LaNelle

another family for a couple of days. My oldest sister Sandra and I had been sleeping on the floor in the second bedroom, so it was nice to sleep in an actual bed.

At the age of eight, it was an important time in my life because another event took place that set the pattern of my disbelief in God. My mother's very close friend Sheryl was dying. She was the most beautiful woman I had ever seen. Even as a small child, I was impressed with her beauty. She had raven black hair and a beautiful smile. I can remember thinking how happy she was in contrast to the miserable life I lived. In my child's mind, she looked like a grown-up version of Snow White from the fairy tale.

When I returned from school, I found my mother crying. Though I had seen her cry many times, this day it was different and it really disturbed me. I asked her what was wrong. She explained that her good friend Sheryl, my beautiful Snow White, might be dying. Mother took me into her room and knelt beside her bed where we prayed for Sheryl. Mother said that if our faith was strong enough, God would heal her and she would get well. I was taught about God and prayer and so I prayed with all the faith I could muster.

Even in these difficult circumstances, I resumed the business of playing and having fun. A few days later, mother was very distraught and I found out that Sheryl had passed away. My mother had not taken the time to explain to a young child that the Lord's will, what He knows is best, was also a factor in prayers such as ours. I could not understand why Sheryl had died and I was very hurt that our prayer did not work.

A few days later, we attended Sheryl's funeral. There was a long procession to her coffin and I thought, "When I get up there, I am going to ask God to restore her life." Everything is so simple in the mind of a child. As we approached the coffin, I asked my mother to lift me up so I could kiss Sheryl goodbye. As mother lifted me, I said, "Please God, let my mother's friend come back to life

21

and live again." Sheryl did not move; she was silent and still.

I was mortified as we watched the coffin being lowered into the ground. I thought, "Maybe my mother is wrong, maybe there is no God. If there is an all-powerful God who cared about us, like my mother said, wouldn't he have brought this beautiful woman back to life?"

So, between my father's actions, the home life I had, and my confusion about this first experience with death, I thought in my little girl mind, that God did not exist, in fact could not exist. Later in life, other events seemed to confirm these thoughts.

At the age of ten, our family was eating ice cream on our old brown couch. My mother asked me for a pillow. As I handed it to her, it hit the tip of my spoon and flicked drops of ice cream on the couch. I didn't know why my father started yelling and hitting me repeatedly on the head. I woke up in my room with my parents standing over my bed. I realized that he had knocked me unconscious.

This attack was one of the only times my father showed remorse after such an act of violence. He finally said repeatedly "I'm sorry." I had heard those words before, and so they had lost all meaning for me. If he had truly been sorry, it would never happen again, but of course I knew it would.

It was not me alone who was abused. One day my sisters and I were getting our once-a-year dresses in a local Sears store. My older sisters and I got separated from our parents. When they found us, our father hit my sisters with his blackjack out in the parking lot. I escaped punishment at the time because I had a broken arm.

We moved again, I was the new "white trash" kid at school, and I definitely looked the part. I had one dress and a pair of tennis shoes that I wore every day. I was underweight and scrawny because there was never much food in our house. The majority of the time I ate white bread with mayonnaise on it. In the sixth grade I weighed only sixty pounds, though I was tall for my age. One day I passed out in a Presbyterian Church yard while walking home from school. I woke up in the hospital and was unhappy to see my father there. Somehow this prompted my parents to re-marry for the third time.

When I was turning eleven, we moved to another apartment on Sepulveda Boulevard in West Los Angeles next to the freeway. I met the neighbors next door – a beautiful woman and a man who looked like a monster. His face looked like melted cheese. I was afraid to be around him. He was actually a very nice man. I learned that he had been in a terrible fire that had disfigured his face and body. At first, I wondered why a woman so lovely would be with someone that looked like that. It taught me a valuable lesson. True beauty comes from within. A very handsome man can be very ugly inside, and another not so handsome can be as pure as gold. This couple had two sons, Johnny and Mark. I had a crush on Johnny. One afternoon while my parents were food shopping Johnny had stopped to talk with me. I was so happy that he paid me any attention. Just then my parents pulled into the parking lot. My father yelled at me to get into the apartment. I replied, "Just a minute." A minute or two later I went in. I could see that my father was very angry. He removed his thin leather belt and repeatedly whipped me on my back until tiny streaks of blood appeared through my little white blouse. My mother and father argued about what he had done. He ordered her to get in the car and me to go to my room and not come out. When they left, I was determined to run away from home. I went to my friend's house as I usually did to have lunch. I told her mother what had happened and she said she was going to call the police. That frightened me because I was afraid of what my father would do if he found out. I ran home as fast as I could and stayed in my room.

The relationship between father and mother was anything but usual. They had actually been divorced and married on three different occasions, and separated more than a dozen times. He had been cheating on my mother since long before I was born, and this continued after they were married. They were either separated or divorced at the time of my birth. My father wanted to name me after his girlfriend Nell, who was my mother's nurse, but mom added the "La" and I was named La Nelle.

My mother tried for years to get away from him. She would run away, a hundred times it seemed, but he would find out where we were. He threatened to kill all of us if she didn't return. I remember once, in his rage, my father took my mother and me in our car to the edge of a cliff. He had one foot on the brake and the other pressing on the gas pedal, revving the engine, all the while cursing and screaming that he was going to drive the car over the edge and kill us. We were screaming and pleading for him not to do it. For a short time, we didn't know if we were going to die or not.

A major frustration for me growing up was our constant moving. We never lived anywhere for very long, so I was never able to form lasting friendships with anyone. I can remember at the age of eighteen trying to count how many times we had moved. Much of the moving was our mother trying to get all of us away from our father, but somehow, he always came back. It was a cruel game of hide and seek with none of the joy found in the children's game.   Each additional act of cruelty heightened my fear and hatred for him.

There Is No God

As I've already said, the horrible experiences in my life only served to convince me that God did not exist. If he did exist, he did not care about me or hear and answer my prayers.

As the years rolled by, life did not get any better. My schooling was hit-and-miss because of our constant moving. I would attend four or five different schools in the course of one year.

Often, we lived in run-down, sometimes cockroach-infested apartments with mattresses on the floor, dishes piled up in the sink and a lot of clutter. My sister Deborah would make bows out of toilet paper to put in our hair. I always felt shuffled around, misplaced and worthless. The feeling was always with me.   I never really felt like I belonged to anything or anyone and was very unhappy. From the age of ten to eighteen, I lived in seven different foster homes.

These were not government subsidized and sponsored foster homes, but homes arranged through friends or a church. Only one of these homes provided any real happiness, affording me with some of the happiest times of my early life. When I think back to a place that I could call "home," it was that beautiful house on Ocean View Avenue in Mar Vista, California. I lived in this home a couple of times with my "sister" Joanne. We have been close friends since the age of 12. We did everything together.   We both had inexpensive cameras and would take what we called "pot shots." One of us would sit on the steps of a mansion in Beverly Hills, or lean against an expensive car, and the other would take a picture. Many times throughout my life she has rescued me in several different ways. She was the one person throughout my life that I loved more than anyone in the world, other than my children.

My First Marriage

At the age of 18, a new boy moved into our town of Simi Valley, California. We had a mutual attraction. His name was Michael. He was from Utah, he was a snow skier, and he rode a Triumph 650 motorcycle. I loved his entire family, and especially his mother. She was soft spoken, kept an immaculate house, and was a phenomenal cook. No one could have asked for a better mother in-law. I nicknamed her "Mama Herd." I wanted to be just like her in every way. However, I think I failed miserably. Mike and I dated for a short while. His father was a Bishop and he married us in their beautiful home. Coming from a dysfunctional home life, I didn't really know what it took to be a wife. I had no example of a working relationship. I wasn't as warm towards him as I should have been. It wasn't his fault. He was a very hard worker and was very good to me. He exercised a lot of patience with me during the three years we were married. Our first born was Sean Christian, our second son was Chad Michael. They were beautiful blonde-haired, blue-eyed boys, and very well behaved. They never gave me any trouble.

After Chad Michael was born, I began having symptoms of headaches, constant thirst, and a never-ending exhaustion. As a child, I had always been frail. My health had always been poor, perhaps aggravated by the abuse and insufficient diet I had received while growing up. Now I was twenty-one years old. I was totally exhausted and had a hard time keeping up with the apartment. I knew something was very wrong with me.

Michael took me to a doctor and I was diagnosed with Type 1 diabetes. They wanted to give me an insulin shot right then but I told the doctor I would rather die than have to take a shot. I learned that I would have to take insulin shots every day to control it. What happens when you tell a person who is terrified of needles and injections that to survive, she has to have shots every day for the rest of her life? I could not even imagine giving myself a shot. Even during the blood tests required to get a marriage license, I had to lie down so I wouldn't faint when I saw the needle.

Three days later Michael carried me into the doctor's office to have my first shot because I was too sick to argue. It was horrifying to take the shots by myself. For the first week using insulin I knocked on every neighbor's door to ask if they could help me. Finally, I learned to do it by myself. Once more, life had knocked me down with a piercing blow. Then things became even more complicated.

My Father's Death

While I was married to Michael, my mother told me my father was dying of cancer and, though they were divorced at the time, he had asked her if she would take care of him. I was very upset when I heard this. I said to her, "You are not going to this, are you?" She took care of him for months, until he became so ill that he could no longer move. He was then transferred to a hospice facility.

Even though I was nine months pregnant with Sean at the time, I flew from Colorado to the hospital in Orem, Utah to see him. What a sight! Imagine a 6' 2" man weighing 70 pounds. Finally, I was the one in control of the situation. He couldn't hurt me anymore and so I was free to tell him just how I felt. I was vicious. I said every vile, nasty, mean and evil thing I could think of. I told him that I hated him and that I hoped he burned in hell for everything he had done to me and my family. I let all of the hate pour out of me, and I told him that he was responsible for my horrible childhood and he was the reason I could not function as an adult. I blamed him for every mistake I had ever made.

To my utter astonishment, in the middle of my tirade he held out his arms and asked me to forgive him. I thought, "What a nerve he had." I told him, "I will never forgive you for all the trauma you put me through." I left the hospital room angry but with some satisfaction that finally I had been able to say all of the things I had felt for so long. About a week later he died.

My sister Deborah went to the funeral just to support our mother, but my other sisters and I did not attend. I didn't even shed a tear. I hated him so much. I was just glad that he was gone. That part of the nightmare was over. My sweet mother deserved to have peace in her life too, something she had not had for many years. "Now," I thought, "maybe I could get on with my life."

Mike and I Divorce

We tried for three years to make our marriage work. We had separated a couple of times, but eventually I gave up. Michael worked the graveyard shift and slept during the day. I had two babies to take care of and was by myself most of the time. Though I felt alone, I really did love him. However, the divorce was more my fault than his.

A long time passed after our divorce. Michael met a lovely girl named Laurel. They married and eventually had eight children. Michael, his wife Laurel, and I, have remained friends for many years. They invited me to Thanksgiving dinner and Michael and I attended our oldest son Sean's high school graduation. I was so happy he married the perfect girl. I love her.

My Second Marriage

At age twenty-two I married again. Throughout my life, I felt that I could not stand up for myself due to fear of punishment or rejection. I was very subservient to my second husband Glenn because of his violent temper. A week after we were married, I discovered I had married a man just like my father. One day I called Mike's mother to get a recipe. Glenn walked in an asked who I was talking to, I told him I was talking to Mike's mom, my former mother in-law. Glenn hung up the phone, slapped me, and said, "You are never talking to those people again." Our short marriage was a nightmare. Immediately, Glenn established many rules for myself and my two sons. He insisted that I do not have friends over while he attended school. If I drank a glass of water, he expected me to wash, dry, and put it away in the cupboard. I could not leave even one utensil in the sink ever. I literally mopped and waxed the kitchen floor daily. On one occasion, he severely injured me when he found dust in the ceiling fan in the bathroom.

Nine months after our marriage I had a third son named Glenn Aaron. During my pregnancy and delivery, there were complications because of my diabetes. Glenn Aaron was adorable and a very sweet baby.

My husband never allowed me to go to the market or anywhere alone, always arranging to be with me. The first time he allowed me to go to the market alone, on my way I stopped at a four way stop in our Volkswagen Beetle. As I proceeded through the intersection, a large motorcycle ran the stop sign and collided with my car. The car spun around. When it came to a stop the passenger side door was open and the baby was not in the car. A lady ran from across the street screaming "Don't look, don't look!" I was afraid the baby was dead. An ambulance came and took Glenn Aaron to a hospital while I followed in a police car. Glenn Aaron had been born October 27th. It was very cold outside at the time, so I had made him a very thick baby quilt. He was wrapped in that quilt at the time of the accident. After doctors examined the baby, his only injury was a little gravel embedded in the top of his head, which happened when he rolled out of the quilt. The quilt saved him from more serious injury.

Chad, Glenn, Sean

Whenever we drove in the car my three sons had to keep their arms folded and could not speak or make any

30

noise. If they did, he would hit them. Once, on a drive to visit my mother, one of the boys giggled and Glenn ordered me to reach back and slap that child. I explained that they were not even talking but had barely made a noise. I said I was not going to punish him. I looked at them with a stare that warned them to be quiet. As I turned my head back around, he backhanded me in the face because I had disobeyed him. He split my upper lip and gave me a bloody nose. We arrived at my mother's house with my face bloodied. He told her we had a minor accident, but my mother knew better. She wanted to call the police but I said, "No, it would just cause more trouble."

Glenn was attending school at the University of Utah. We lived in the Medical Towers. There was a large circular playground in the center of the complex. Here, the children could play on the swings, slides, and in the sand with their mothers while the fathers attended classes. I was the only wife not allowed to participate in these activities with my children. He was insanely jealous, and feared losing me. He thought another man might approach me and talk to me. He thought I would perhaps leave him for someone else.

His attempts to control me became unbearable. He tried to brainwash me but was never successful. All of the rules, suspicions, and recriminations only added to my lack of self-esteem and confidence. Whenever he got angry with the boys, he would punish them in various cruel ways. On one occasion, Chad, who was only two, got into my makeup bag when I was at a women's meeting. When I returned home, Glenn Senior was crying. He had whipped Chad with a wire hanger. When I saw my little boy, he had welts all over his bottom and legs. Glenn said "I lost my temper." I told him if he ever touched my boys again,

I would leave him. He never was able to control his temper.

One weekend we were taking a trip to see his family in California. We hadn't had any arguments or problems, when suddenly, somewhere in the desert between Las Vegas and Los Angeles, he pulled the car over to the side of the road and told us all to get out. Then he drove off and left us. I called my "sister" Joanne and she picked us up and took us to her home. When I returned to Utah, I filed for divorce. The only car we had was his Volkswagen. Again, I was left with no car, no money, and I had to find work. We stayed with Joanne until I could find a place to live.

We separated eleven times during our three-year marriage. Each time we separated, I had to find a new apartment and a new job. I had no money and all the children to care for. I moved where I could, sometimes out of state, to stay with friends or family.

Our marriage ended in a bitter divorce. I wanted out so badly that I didn't contest anything. I left with just my clothes and my children.

During the divorce, Glenn demanded custody of our child. During the hearing, he constantly lied. He told the judge I was uneducated and didn't care about the children getting an education. He omitted the fact that the children were being home schooled by an accredited teacher. After hours of lawyers battling, the judge called Glenn Aaron back into his chambers and asked him who he wanted to be with. He said, "I want to live with my mother." I was granted custody of our son and moved to Provo, Utah, but Glenn kept trying to pursue me.

Over the years, many of my friends who saw the movie *Sleeping with the Enemy* starring Julia Roberts, asked if that movie had been written about my marriage. I was about a millimeter away from a nervous breakdown and worried about my ex-husband who was livid about losing custody of our son.

After my divorce, I did whatever I could to care for my children. I went back to the menial jobs like the ones I had worked prior to my second marriage. I took jobs that were available for an uneducated single mom. I cleaned houses, waitressed, did professional sewing, and cooked for other people. I never asked for alimony or child support from either Michael or Glenn. I found myself moving my children from place to place because of various circumstances. A few times, I entered into relationships so I could better care for the three boys, but those situations always ended in disaster. No matter where I moved, Glenn would always find me.

During this time, I moved several times between California and Utah. While I was living in Provo, someone gave me a bicycle and I got a job at a local restaurant. I was on the late shift and I rode the bike to and from work. Joanne had started college at Brigham Young University and stayed with the boys most of the time while I worked. She was always there for me. Finally, I secretly moved to American Fork and didn't tell Glenn so he could not find us.

My Son Is Kidnapped

A few years later, as Glenn Aaron was turning eight, his father tricked my mother into telling him where we were living. Our son was riding his bike with a friend in front of our house one day when Glenn drove up in a "beater" car dressed like a cowboy. He jumped out of the car, knocked our son's friend off of his bike, and grabbed Glenn Aaron. His friend ran home and told his mother what had happened. She came screaming to my house and repeated what her son had told her. I ran outside to the graveled driveway and fell to my knees in shock. I called the police. Eventually they exhausted their efforts to locate him. Two weeks later I received a telegram saying that my former husband had taken our son, and I was never going to see him again. Ten years later my missing child ran away from his father. He searched for me for months and located me in Sherman Oaks, California where we were finally reunited.

Years later, before Glenn's death, he confessed that his violent treatment of my sons and myself was motivated by his insane jealousy. The thought of the relationship I once had with Michael that had resulted in the birth of these two beautiful blonde boys was more than he could handle. They represented a constant reminder to him of that previous marriage. He said he could never be second.

David Soul

In 1975, a new TV series featuring David Soul premiered and I began watching it. I had seen him in other TV shows and movies in the past. He looked like an angel to me. There was a nice spirit about him, so I went to 20th Century Fox Studios to meet him. I walked right onto the lot like I belonged there. I located where they were filming the series and walked right up to him with a loaf of homemade banana bread. We talked for a few minutes and he invited me into his trailer. I asked him if he could play his guitar for me. He said, "I am in a serious relationship." I replied, "I did not come here to sleep with you." He told me if I was ever in the area again to come see him. A lot of actors have girls who follow them around. They are called "groupies." I was not one of them! David and I had a strange relationship for several years. We would come in and out of each other's lives periodically. I will always care a great deal about him. I had previously dated well-known actors in the past - Hugh O'Brian, Ben Murphy, and others.

Sarah (LaNelle) with Hugh O'Brian

I never cared about fame or fortune. If I truly loved someone I could live in a tent and he could work in a gas station. His mind, heart, and spirit were what I cared about. Men were always trying to buy me, but my love was never for sale.

I moved between Utah and California more than a few times. While living in Los Angeles, I discovered that clients appreciated my work and men found me attractive. I was able to find jobs serving at parties for wealthy people in Beverly Hills and Bel Air. The money was better than I had been able to make doing anything else. I have to admit there was a certain excitement involved at attending the parties even if it was in the capacity of a servant.

I rented an apartment in Beverly Hills on Doheny Drive. It was a single apartment with barely enough room for my three boys and myself. Sean and Chad slept on the Murphy bed that folded up into the wall. Glenn Aaron slept on a small love seat that had no cushions, and I slept on the floor. The apartment was supposed to be for just one person, but the manager, Anita, took mercy on us and allowed me to have my three boys there. Anita and I became very close friends and have remained so to this day.

The job serving at parties had evolved into a household cook position for a prominent family in Beverly Hills. I had worked hard during the last few years earning a reputation for gourmet cooking and maintaining their homes. This eventually landed me jobs working for several well-known celebrities. During the day, I worked in mansions, rode in limousines and was surrounded by glamorous people. At night I served at parties in their homes while my friend Anita watched my children. My plan was to save enough money to get out of Los Angeles. I had too many dark memories to remain there. However, the black cloud that always hovered over my life grew darker yet.

Sarah (LaNelle), Audition for TV Show

36

The "Proposition"

The owner of the apartment building where I lived was a well-to-do foreigner. He knew that I would need extra money to raise three children alone. One day, after serving for a party at his home, he approached me with a proposition. Free rent, a decorated apartment and certain other "privileges" if I would just be "friendly" to his brother who had seen me at the party. I knew that being "friendly" meant sleeping with him, and even though I was alone and needed help, I would never do anything like that, not even to feed my children or for any other reason.

When I turned down my landlord's "generous" offer he began threatening my life. It shocked me how fast things could turn on me so quickly and so completely, but it seemed the story of my life. Just when my life began to look promising, I got knocked down again.

My landlord continued to pressure me and threatened to have me killed if I didn't give in. I became depressed and desperate. As my problems came to a head, in a moment of complete despair, I sat on the front porch of my apartment and cried and cried, trying to think of how I was going to get out of this mess. I must have presented quite a picture, with my head buried in my arms, sobbing, because while I was sitting there crying, as if in the script of a movie, a big limousine pulled up. A man got out and asked, "Are you okay?" I lied and said yes, but, then broke down and told him the complete tragic story. He told me he was a Hollywood producer and had a very large estate in Belair. He and his lady friend had a baby, and he would pay me $2500 a month to live in their home, cook for them and care for the infant.

"Maybe there is a God," I thought. One month's salary would be all I needed to get out of Los Angeles and find some peace and a safer place for my sons. The one catch was that I could not bring my children with me to the new job. Even though the thought of sending the boys away was a tremendous sacrifice, I felt that it would only be temporary, just until I had earned enough money to relocate and start over.

By this time Sean and Chad's father, Michael, had remarried. He and his new wife welcomed the chance to have the two boys stay with them temporarily. Glenn Aaron, my youngest son, then seven years old, went to live with a kind clergyman's family in West L.A. When all of the boys were placed safely in good homes, I was free to take the job that I hoped would lead to a new start in life for all of us. All I wanted to do was get away, get out of Los Angeles and California.

As could easily be imagined from the way challenges had been going in my life, it soon became apparent that all was not as it seemed to be in the new job. Yes, this man was indeed a producer, but after I moved in I found out that he was also one of the largest cocaine dealers in Hollywood. I learned that he had been a talented movie producer but had decided that the easy way to make more money was by dealing drugs.

Movie stars and other "Hollywood People" came to the house at all hours of the day and night. Most often, they would disappear into the producer's bedroom with him and emerge a short time later and leave.

My suspicions were confirmed at a huge party he threw when Hollywood celebrities started using the white powder he had placed in dishes around the room. It was cocaine. But I did not care, it was none of my business. With my lifestyle I had never even taken baby aspirin.

I did not care, that is, until one night not long after the party, I was alone in the house with their baby. I was talking on the phone with my foster sister, Joanne, about what I was going to do. I had not yet been paid anything, he always came up with excuses, and my circumstances were not improving.

All of a sudden, someone picked up the receiver on another phone in the house. I asked, "Who is this, who's on this phone?" The voice on the other end said, "Hang up or we'll cut your throat." I was terrified and ran out of the house, making my way to a few of the neighbors' homes. I banged on their doors and yelled hysterically that someone was going to kill me and we had to save the baby who was still in the house. Either no one was home or they were all convinced that I was a crazy woman loose in the neighborhood. Maybe no one cared. Either way no doors opened for me that night. Finally, a van came down the street. I flagged it down and quickly explained the situation. They drove off and called the police. Shortly before this incident an entire family had been murdered in Beverly Hills because they were about to testify in court against a very powerful person. The police thought these might be the same killers. The police cars and helicopters arrived in minutes and caught the men who had entered the house. They were druggies looking for cocaine. The police also arrested the producer when he arrived home because of the cocaine they discovered in the house. I had been there almost six weeks, and now this disaster. I had never been paid. It seemed the story of my life.

Of course, I left with no money and nowhere to go. I thought, "This is it. This is the last straw. Nothing I do ever works out." When all seemed hopeless, Shaun, a movie editor with whom I had become acquainted while working at the producer's home, offered to let me stay at his place, no strings attached. He was a friend and client of the producer, though he said he no longer used cocaine. He had been kind to me, and somehow, I felt I could trust him when he offered me a safe place to stay. Besides, I had nowhere else to go.

While staying at Shaun's place, I tried to help by keeping his apartment clean and cooking for him. Our relationship was purely platonic. He had bailed me out of a tough spot, so I thought a little cooking and housekeeping was the least I could do. A few days later while cleaning up, I discovered a stash of cocaine. I was shocked and angry, because I had believed him when he told me he had stopped using the drug. My anger propelled me on as I flushed the entire bag down the toilet. When he came home later that day, I confronted him with my discovery and told him what I had done with it. When he realized that thousands of dollars' worth of cocaine had been flushed down the toilet, he was furious. I was furious too because he had lied to me. As I scolded him, he pushed me into the fireplace and stormed out of the apartment.

When he didn't come back after four days, I finally called the studio where he worked. The person answering the phone told me that Shaun had locked himself in the editing room and no one had seen him for the entire time. I was concerned and upset. I stormed down to the studio. I banged on the door to the editing room and threatened to call the police if he didn't open up. When he finally did, I was saddened to see huge dark circles under his eyes. He was shaking and obviously on a cocaine binge. All he said was, "Leave me alone," and closed the door. I went back to his apartment.

It didn't matter what I did, I always felt like my life was a total failure. My existence held only unhappiness and misery. Life had lost all appeal for me. I became so upset that I was not thinking clearly. I had no idea what I was going to do. I walked around in a daze. All these emotions made me believe that the only alternative left for me was suicide. I was actually hoping that there was no life after death, that way I would not have to remember anything about my life. I was in tears as I cleaned his condo. I was playing a 45 RPM record that I set to play repeatedly. It kept repeating the words, "Do it or die." I had always tried to improve my life, however I seemed to fail at every attempt. I could never "do it," so like the song said, I thought it best to just "die."

Sarah (LaNelle), 1979

The Suicide

On that fateful day, I decided I could not go on any longer. I could not trust people, I hated life in general, and I especially hated MY life. I could not get rid of the thought that my children deserved better than what I could give them. I was not even able to take care of myself. I felt useless and I thought it would be best for everyone if I just went away. Permanently.

I had sprained my ankle a few months earlier roller skating in Beverly Hills, and the doctor had given me a prescription for pain pills. I was very much into health foods so I put the medication on the shelf unopened. The day I decided to take my life I swallowed the entire bottle of Tylenol with codeine. I may have taken a few other things also. I don't remember.

Apparently, though I do not remember it, as I was losing consciousness, I called my sister Deborah, who had moved to Utah. She said that I had asked her to tell our mother that I loved her and that I forgave her. Subconsciously I must have felt that our mother should have done more to protect us from our father, although now I know that she had done everything she could.

After I said those things, I collapsed. Because of my slurred speech, and the words I was saying, then when I didn't respond to her anymore, my sister knew something was very wrong. She called the L.A. police department. They made an attempt to get into Shaun's building by yelling at the neighbors to open the outside entrance so they could reach Shaun's apartment. They ran down the long hallway and kicked his door in. They rushed in, and I saw them run over to something on the floor. I was out of my body and looking down on everything from somewhere near the ceiling. I began to realize that it was my body lying on the floor. The EMTs started taking vitals on it, and one of them said, "no heartbeat, no pulse...she's dead." My face was very pale and my lips were blue. It was strange but I didn't think of the body on the floor as being "me," or even a part of "me." As I looked at it, the body on the floor was nothing more to me than a lump of clay.

I listened to their conversations and watched them quickly walk from room to room. They had not yet determined what had happened. One police officer went into one of the bedrooms and was going through things there. Another officer walked into the bathroom and started going through the medicine cabinet. Under the sink, he found my medical bag and my insulin. He yelled out, "I think she might be a diabetic," and continued looking through everything under the sink. While he was doing this in the bathroom, one of the paramedics took the phone out of my hand and hung it up. It rang almost immediately. The paramedic picked it up and asked, "Do you have any information on this girl that is here. We found a dead body." I thought it was a very strange thing for him to say. I was not dead. I could hear and see everything perfectly. I could also hear through the wire and heard the man who had called say he didn't know anything.

In fact, as I think back on that night, I find it strange and wonderful that while all of this was happening, I was able to see everything all at the same time, regardless of where it took place. Walls of brick or wood did not seem to hinder my vision at all. That night it all seemed very natural and didn't even draw my attention. Everything that was happening fascinated me. All of the activity, in some removed, distant way had something to do with me. But it hadn't fully registered yet.

While the one paramedic was talking on the phone, the other one was still working on my body. When the one hung up the phone, the other one said, "She hasn't been gone very long, her body is still warm. Let's try to revive her. Get the paddles out."

When they said this and started trying to revive me, I became upset when they shocked my body and I saw it lift up off the ground and drop back down. I tried talking to them. I said, "Leave it alone." I did not want to go back

43

into that clump of clay. I think I said it twice. They ignored me and I lost interest.

Instantly, I was no longer floating in the air above my body. I was standing at the edge of a beautiful silver lake.

CHAPTER 2

૱

The World of Spirits

"Beautiful Beyond Description"

The Silver Lake

The move from my previous location had been instantaneous. In less than a blink of an eye I found myself in an entirely different world from the one I had inhabited since birth, a world unlike anything I had ever seen or had ever imagined. In the distance and all around me were magnificent hills covered with trees, grass and flowers of every hue imaginable and unimagined. There was a large and beautiful lake to my right. The surface of the lake looked to me like crushed diamonds or liquid silver.

Everyone who knows me knows that I have an intense, almost irrational fear of water. I cannot swim a stroke and I am terrified of water and the possibility of drowning. Once, when I was young, on the only family vacation we ever took, my father decided that he would cure me of my fear of water and teach me to swim all at the same time. He pushed me off of a pier into a lake. I swallowed water, panicked and felt as if I were going to drown. My father only succeeded in intensifying my fear of water. I have not even been able to walk around the deep end of a swimming pool for fear of accidentally falling in. Only in the last few years have I been able to get into a hot tub without having an anxiety attack. So, when I say that I was standing beside a lake without any fear whatsoever, this is extremely significant.

My intense fear of water had always been a part of me but now it was inexplicably gone. My fear turned to fascination for the body of water that was before me. It was beautiful. As I leaned over the edge to look into the lake, I realized that I could see through the crystal-clear water for what seemed like miles to the bottom of the lake. I don't know how deep it was, but it was very, very deep. There were tremendous numbers and varieties of fishes swimming through the underwater foliage that was everywhere waving in the currents. The fishes and the foliage were of the most vivid colors, very bright, and there were so many different hues.

The only way to compare the colors I saw there would be to say that the color spectrum we know in this world is muted and dull, as if seen through some sort of glass that subdues the colors and makes them less vivid. To describe our vision in this life as vastly limited is an understatement. Here we are able to see only a tiny fraction of what I saw there. Not only are the colors like nothing we can imagine, the words do not exist in our vocabulary that adequately describe the beauty of that world.

As I stood there at the edge of this magnificently beautiful lake, I was enticed by the water and wanted to fall into it and allow it to engulf me. Instinctively I knew that the water was somehow alive and that it would not harm me. I wasn't aware of how this knowledge came to me; I just knew. The feeling lasted only for a moment, and then the rest of my surroundings captured my attention.

Beautiful Surroundings

Beautiful flowers and vegetation unknown in our world were everywhere. The colors of the flowers were so vibrant, but impossible for me to describe because they were so different from anything I had ever seen. I have no names for the flowers. The grass felt like soft, plush velvet, of a bright, vivid green color. Never in my life have I seen anything in nature to match the beauty of that world. In the meadow, the trees were full and plush. From the lake, I looked to my left and saw a hill blanketed with trees that resembled weeping willows. All I had to do was think that I would like to be there, and instantly I was on the top of the hill.

I realized that I no longer had any limitations with my vision. My eyesight was enhanced and so sharp that I could literally see for miles. As I looked out in the far distance, objects appeared to grow closer, like zooming in with a telephoto lens. Distance was not an issue any more. These new abilities fascinated me and I just stood there looking around for a while. The hill was even more beautiful up close than it was from a distance.

The sky was a beautiful deep, rich blue. There appeared to be objects floating in the sky that looked like huge, puffy clouds. On closer inspection, I could see that they were actually formations of swirling light with a cloud-like appearance.

I had no thoughts about my earthly material possessions, not my dear children, or anyone else that I may have loved. I could not think of anything I had left behind. I could only appreciate how wonderful it was to be here. A tremendous feeling of peace came over me.

My newly acquired senses soon made me aware that the grove of trees where I stood, and the plants and grass around me, were alive and could communicate with me, and that they not only knew who I was, but were happy that I was there with them. They did not think as we do, but they nonetheless seemed to have feelings and a form of intelligence. Even though the intelligence of the plants was different from our own, it was still very real. I stood there for a while feeling the love for me that radiated from these forms of life. I now saw them from a completely different perspective. That was when I started to ask, and think of, questions about this new world. I first asked, "Where am I?" and quickly went on from there.

Questions Answered

During this time, it became clear to me that the way my mind operated was very different. It was not the same as it had been on earth. When we think in mortality, we are limited to one thought at a time. In this world of spirits, I could ask hundreds of questions at the same time and receive the answers all at once, and I could assimilate everything perfectly. I was amazed at the expanded capabilities of my spirit-mind. I stood there for quite a while asking questions and receiving the answers I desired. For example:

Where did all these spirit beings live?

They dwelt in beautiful houses with elegant furnishings. Some of them had ornately carved wooden staircases. Others had crystal floors with living multi-colored flowers that I could see as I looked through the beautiful rooms. Most of these homes were trimmed in gold. Oddly enough, there were no bedrooms. Spirits never tire, so they require no sleep.

Surrounding every home were miles and miles of beautiful grassy hills, clustered with magnificent trees, flowers, and streams. If a spirit wanted to visit the city, they need only to think it and they would instantly be there.

Questions and Answers

Do Spirit Beings interact with those living on earth? Are they involved with our lives? Are they able to return and visit familiar people and places?

Our loved ones and friends who have passed on are very much involved in our lives. They are actually with us and help us more than we know. They talk to us constantly. Often when impressions come to your mind, for example, "Don't park your car here, it might not be safe," or "Don't go with that person," and you feel uneasy for some reason. Many random thoughts that seem to come out of the blue are often from them. This is one small example about how they perform as our guardian angels.

Spirits are beings just like us but without a physical (mortal) body. They have the ability to revisit where they lived while on earth. They attend special family occasions such as the birth of a new child, weddings, anniversaries, and funerals. Every person who passes away is permitted to attend their own funeral. If your spiritual eyes could be opened, you would see spirits all around you. Some of these might be your ancestors.

On rare occasions, and with special permission, they can reveal themselves so a family member or person who needs help can see and hear them. If you want to see an example of this, see the movie "Cokeville Miracle." This movie portrays the events that led up to, and followed, the bombing at the Cokeville, Wyoming elementary school that occurred on Friday, May 16, 1986. Each child described seeing angels coming down from the ceiling. They told the children where to stand so that they would be protected from the explosion. The angels then formed a circle in the air to confine the explosion and to protect the children from the debris. Later, when going through photos of relatives who had passed away long ago, they were able to identify the spirit beings who helped them.

As I observed and understood my surroundings, even more answers to thoughts and questions flooded my mind.

A basic similarity exists between the world of mortality and the world of spirits. It seems familiar at first glance, but closer inspection revealed significant differences. I also learned that time, as we think of it on earth, did not exist there. This is all very difficult to explain with our limited human vocabulary. Unless you have been there, and seen it, or even had a small glimpse, the experience is hard to explain. I learned to call it a spirit world. In this realm, there are no seconds, minutes, hours or days. All of our senses are heightened. Our sense of time, vision, hearing, and smelling have no limits. There is a complete freedom of thought, of vision, and of all the senses as far as I could tell.

A fragrance exists in the world of spirits that is incredible and unlike anything earthly that I have ever smelled. The fragrance is not like any perfume or the scent of a flower. It is actually more than that. The scent was happy, peaceful, restful and calming. This fragrance made me feel alive and wonderful, just as everything else did here. Every sense is accentuated and contributes to the feeling of peace and happiness that permeates this amazing place.

The Dream Cottage

As I stood on the hill asking questions and receiving answers, after what seemed like a few moments I paused to look at something that caught my eye off in the distance. It was a beautiful cottage in a valley far, far away. It was so very beautiful and perfect. It was surrounded with trees and flowers and little streams with silvery water running all around the land. It fit best the description of a fairytale cottage. It had a round-topped door with what looked like a cobblestone path leading up to it and what appeared to be a soft thatched roof.

Gazing upon this scene the thought came to me that I would love to live in such a house as this little cottage, and immediately the answer came, "You can, you can live in whatever type of building or house that would make you happy." The decision of my living circumstances was primarily up to me, within the limits of whatever I had earned.

Animals in The Spirit World

As I looked at the cottage and admired how pretty and perfect it was, I noticed a dog walking along a path. The dog appeared to be an Irish setter, with long dark hair. I was somewhat surprised and thought to myself, "There are pets here?" The response that filled my head was, "Yes, there are animals here of all kinds, some of them were pets to people on earth."

I was made to understand that if a person had animals that they loved and cared for in life, and if the animals also loved them and wanted to be with them, they could then be together in this place.

As I looked at the dog, it seemed to sense it and looked back at me and I could hear and feel its thoughts of love and recognition. It surprised me a little and then immediately I understood that the spirits of animals and people could communicate with and understand each other the same way I had communicated with the plants earlier, that is, telepathically. The difference being that the animals communicated on a higher level than the trees and grass but still well below the level of my thoughts.

I was also given to understand that on earth the animals could understand people but that our ability to understand them had been taken away. The thoughts of animals are simple, like the thoughts of a child, and they have personalities and desires as well.

One of the reasons animals exist on earth is to help us learn to love. There are some people who have not developed the ability to love other people but are capable of loving animals. I also understood that the lives of animals are precious, and those who take the lives of animals without cause, or are cruel to them, will have serious consequences.

The City of Light

I saw in the distance what looked like numerous cities filled with beautiful buildings. The cities seemed to glow, as if light was coming from them. I soon realized that what I saw was one enormous city with millions of people. Looking down at the city, I was again able to use my unlimited vision and see it as though I were standing nearby.

As I remained on the top of the hill surveying the city before me, I became aware that I was not clothed, yet my state of undress did not concern me in the least. I had no thoughts of being seen by others, even though I knew there were people in the city.

When I thought about the clothing, it was revealed to me that I had not passed through the barrier, or "film," that separated this world from the mortal world. If I had passed through the "film," someone would have brought me a robe to wear. I understood that the "film" is like a transparent, thin wall of some fine matter that is used to separate things in the two different worlds. Passing through the "film" prevents one from returning to earth life.

I understood that whenever a person passes away, no matter what their status or situation was on earth, they will be greeted by someone who will assist them. The robe given identifies the wearer as a new arrival and is called a "new spirit entrant robe." These robes differed from the robes worn by other spirits that had been in the spirit world for a longer time. In that way, when someone newly arrived is greeted, they are recognized and received with a warm welcome.

The robes worn by others also identified them as having some authority or as an indication of the work they performed. I understood that there was perfect order there. The assignments or responsibilities of an individual were chosen or agreed to by that person. Some were asked to perform certain tasks, but the choice was always theirs. Everything was voluntary, and there was never any force.

As I was viewing the city, I noticed the streets and paths were all lined with flowers and trees. Beautiful fountains were present that sprayed the silvery water I had seen earlier at the lake. As the water sprayed into the air it appeared as a million glistening, sparkling diamonds too beautiful to describe with words.

The city itself was very similar to our world, with some exceptions. One obvious exception was that there were no cars. Everyone walked or occasionally "glided" to their destinations.

Another major difference, especially from the big city where I had lived, was that everything was immaculate. There was no dirt or trash in the streets, as we have come to see in many of our earthly cities. There were no curbs or gutters, and the streets and many of the smaller walkways seemed to be made out of some kind of flat paving stone. There were beautiful flowers everywhere, lining the rock ways and fountains and streams. The scenery was enhanced with beautiful, perfectly trimmed shrubbery and hedges, making it all very lovely and pleasing to look at.

I was excited and anxious to go down into the city and to be a part of the happiness and love that I felt existed there. I was not to be given that opportunity.

The Buildings

The buildings previously in the distance now appeared close up. They were magnificent. They were not tall buildings. The tallest stood maybe three or four stories high and they were of various designs and architectural styles.

One of the most common designs reminded me a little of Hearst Castle in California. I once watched a television special tour of it with its marble floors, columns, pools and fountains. Some of the buildings I saw in the spirit world had a slight resemblance to that structure. I feel it is important to note that I saw no statues or paintings or artwork of any kind other than beautifully carved furniture in the buildings, unlike the Hearst Castle with its elaborate furnishings. And yet, even the beauty of Hearst Castle pales in comparison to any of the buildings I saw in the city. The buildings and the crystal pools of water within the city were beyond anything that can be seen on this planet.

The buildings have the appearance of a pinkish-white alabaster or marble so thin that it appeared almost to be transparent. At least as I concentrated on one of the beautiful buildings, I could see right through its walls. Inside, I could see columns and steps; I could also see many rooms and corridors. The corridors were very wide and full of people. Fifty people could have easily stood shoulder to shoulder across the width. The rooms were even larger and filled with hundreds of people.

Even though I had come to disbelieve in a life after death and all that was involved with that belief, I had assumed if there was a heaven it would be beautiful beyond imagination. That was surely an apt description of the world I had happened upon, and yet one of the concepts I had learned while asking questions on the hill previously, was that this place, beautiful beyond words, was not heaven. This was only a waiting place for the spirits of people who have departed the earth and who are waiting for a later time when they will be assigned to other places or kingdoms. I came to understand that these other places were kingdoms of glory, while this spirit world was not, and therefore were infinitely more beautiful than this place.

I learned that this spirit world, including the city I was admiring, had different parts or sections, and that the future homes of these departed spirits would also be in kingdoms that varied in beauty and glory, each being more beautiful and glorious than the one before. The highest is the kingdom called "The Holy City," where God the Father and Jesus Christ actually dwell.

At the point when the spirit separates from the mortal body, the center dark circle represents the earth. The first circle surrounding the earth represents the dark tunnel that many people who have gone through an NDE describe passing through. The second circle is the beginning area of coming into the light. 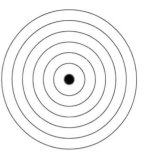 The third circle is the spirit world or paradise where departed beings dwell and will remain until the day of the resurrection. The fourth circle is the lowest region where unrepentant liars, adulterers, and murders reside. The fifth circle represents the good people of the earth who were blinded from the truth of God's teachings by either the craftiness or wrong influence of others and were still unwilling to accept the higher laws of God.

Each circle or sphere becomes brighter and more glorious than the previous one. The last three rings contain several levels or areas that the sons and daughters of our Father in Heaven inherit for eternity.

The very last circle is the highest Kingdom where God the Father and His Son Jesus Christ dwell. It is called the Holy City. Only the children of the Earth that live the higher laws of God and overcome the world and seek to become more like Christ while in this worldly state will live with God and Christ in that highest realm. Yet even the lowest of Kingdoms will be more glorious than the magnificent Spirit World I presently stood in. It gave me great comfort to understand a little more about how merciful and loving our Father in Heaven is.

I also learned that they refer to God the Father as our Heavenly Father and I learned that we are His children. I learned that He and Jesus Christ were two separate glorified beings. They are one in purpose, but not both in one body. Christ sits on the right-hand side of God the Father on His throne. The Holy Ghost has no physical body but is a spirit, a part of the Godhead. It is He who testifies to us of the truth.

Having seen the beauty of the waiting place for spirits, I cannot even imagine how beautiful the home of Jesus must be. I would gladly have stayed in the world I witnessed forever, so wonderful and glorious it was to me.

The People and Activities in the City

I could feel the love that flowed between the people as they exchanged greetings and conversed with each other. The spaces between the buildings were very park-like and spacious. I saw people gathered together in small groups of family and friends and I understood that most activities were done within these same groups. Watching and learning these things, I was excited and anxious to go down into the city and to be a part of the happiness and love that existed there, but I was not to be given that opportunity.

There were many people in the city, and now I noticed the details of their apparel. As a child, and then on rare occasions as an adult, when I took time to think about it, I assumed that people in heaven would wear white. At least that was the way heaven was depicted in all of the paintings I had seen. However, I observed that while many do choose white, others wore beautiful pastel robes. Both men and women wore the same clothing: robes made of a shimmering fabric akin to silk but much softer. The fabric almost glowed and seemed alive with extraordinary colors. The robes were long, down to the ankle, and slit a little up the side almost to the knee. The people wore cummerbunds of differing soft pastel colors around the waist and long shawls that went over the shoulders.

Something else I noticed were a couple of young men wearing dark suits. While visually it stood out, at the time it seemed quite natural and not out of place at all. It came into my mind that these young men may have been given permission to visit relatives in mortality. They wore suits, perhaps ones that they were buried in, so they would be recognized by their family.

After noticing the clothing, I saw that the people themselves gave off a light and seemed to actually glow. The brightness varied from person to person, and a few were of a different, more golden hue. When I noticed the light and the difference in illumination between people, a question formed in my mind. Immediately it came to me that this light was in direct proportion to how each individual had lived their life on earth. Spirits can see how an individual had lived, and this was reflected in the brightness of their countenance.

The "Kitchen"

Looking down a long hall in one of the buildings, there seemed to be a lot of activity in a very large room. The women there seemed to be having a lot of fun laughing and talking as they went about their work. They were not being loud or boisterous, their communication was done quietly. I could see that they took pleasure in what they were doing. They were having a wonderful time.

I realized that they were preparing something to eat. Some of the women were slicing what appeared to be some kind of fruit. The pieces were arranged on crystal platters. Other women were arranging what looked like little wafers of a cake-like bread. I watched as one of the women tasted a wafer as she placed them on the platter. I could see the pleasure she had as she ate it, and I wished that I could experience that too. Immediately, one was in my mouth. It reminded me of baklava. More than just a taste or a flavor, eating the wafer made me feel good and happy all at the same time. The taste was intense as was everything else in this place. As I watched this activity, I was impressed that people ate more for pleasure than for sustenance.

The "Library"

Looking along another corridor I noticed people going in and out of another large room. It was a beautiful library. Row after row of huge books were on shelves along all of the walls. I would estimate that the books were about five or six inches thick and perhaps twelve to fourteen inches high. They were beautifully bound. The bindings of the books were dark brown and there was carving or embossing on the front. People stood at ornate, intricately carved desks or tables, studying and reading.

The people did not read these books as we would. As they opened them up, the books would speak and show moving illustrations of whatever subject one was studying. They learned more rapidly with this unique tool than by reading one word at a time as we do.

I had seen people sitting on the lawns and stone-like benches as they engaged in conversation. It was here that I noticed that there were no chairs. As I pondered this, I was impressed with the understanding that chairs were not really necessary here, unless used in certain types of work. People do not grow tired and so they have no need to sit and rest.

I would like to mention that I heard beautiful music playing. I did not see the instruments, but the music sounded like it could have come from harps and flutes, but I can't be sure. The music was indeed ethereal and soothing. It offered a lovely background to the many activities in which these people were participating.

A Person Repenting

After this, I glanced quickly through another building, generally seeing the same kind of activities. In one room I saw something that caught my attention.

The room was not very large, especially compared to the others I had seen and there appeared to be only one person in the room. In it there was a large screen that seemed to take up one of the walls. It was not like a big TV screen or even a computer screen, not really a screen at all. I can only describe it as being like a transparent screen made out of a gel or water that stayed stationary. It was large and oblong with rounded corners. As I concentrated on the screen, I could see that there was a man in it, or rather the image of a man.

As I focused on the image of the man in the screen for a moment, I was given to understand that the person I saw was still alive and living on the earth and that this screen was a view of his spirit-self. The only person I saw in the room was a man working at a module or console in front of the screen. He was sitting in a chair-like seat that seemed to be a molded part of the console.

While I was watching this scene, the man seated in front of the screen removed a long colored shaped object from one part of the module. It was about four or five inches long and about an inch in diameter. It was flat on one end, pointed on the other, glowed slightly and was very beautiful. He then placed the object into an opening on the console. He repeated this process a few more times with other objects of different colors but all the same shape.

As I saw this happening, I asked in my mind what he was doing at that console. The answer presented to me was that this man's life, the one whose image I saw, was being revised.

This man was repenting, and what he had done was literally being wiped off the screen. This screen reflected the alteration in his spirit. I immediately understood that this is the "book of life," as referred to in the scriptures. Everything that a person says, does, or thinks from the time they are born to the day they die is recorded in their "spiritual DNA," not written down in a book by some heavenly being, as we may think.

I now understood the concept that because of these recordings on our "spiritual DNA," we will be able to look at another person's spirit there in the spirit world and completely read most of their life. The light or glow I had noticed coming from the people earlier was a part of this recording, and I saw that if I concentrated a little harder, I could read the entire life history of any person on which I focused.

I understood that the more righteous or God-like a person had been on earth, or the more good they had done by trying to help others, the brighter would be his or her light in the spirit world. The only parts of a person's life that would not be seen or read were those they had repented of, the way the man on the screen was doing. A person having repented may still remember the deleted segments of his life, but they would be kept from others. I also became aware that there was no casual interest in "looking into" other people's lives.

Another concept I learned is that it is far easier to repent or change our lives in the mortal world than it is after passing into the spirit world. When we make the transition called death, which is referred to there as the "new birth," we take with us our attitudes, passions, desires, habits, qualities and character. We really don't change at all. Everything that makes us who we are comes with us as a part of our essence or "spiritual DNA."

Our thoughts, words, actions, and experiences, from the very beginning help us to become who we really are. However, once we are in the spirit world, all of our emotions and attitudes become greatly intensified thereby increasing the difficulty involved in changing them. I was also informed that if this man on the screen again committed these same sins he was repenting of, the parts that had been removed would be replaced, and all that had been erased would once again be present in his "recording."

As these thoughts and explanations came into my mind, I became frightened. There were parts of my life I definitely did not want others to see. And now, in dismay, I realized I could not hide anything from anyone.

My Life's Review

At that moment I started thinking about everything I had done in my life. As the thoughts of my life formed in my head, a window seemed to open before me, and my life's review began.

A panoramic window opened like a scroll in front of me. It was like a fast-forward video recording showing my entire life from birth until the moment I arrived in the spirit world. It only took seconds, and yet I was doing more than just watching the events of my life pass by. With each event I not only saw my actions, but I heard the thoughts I was thinking and felt what I was feeling at the time. I was re-living each experience, only this time I could see everything else that was happening around me as well. I could see and feel what those people that I interacted with were seeing and feeling. I could actually feel their pain or joy and understand what they were thinking. For me, this was not a pleasant experience.

There were some good things I had done in life, but very few. I began to feel sick and full of pain because of the choices I had made. These "pains of the heart" I had inflicted upon others was a great lesson for me.

Despair set in. I felt sure I would never be able to undo any of my misdeeds. As I viewed my life, there was no doubt in me about what was good or bad. I could no longer lie to myself or to anyone else about my feelings or motives. The worst parts of the review were when I had intentionally hurt someone. Somehow, I now felt my angry emotions of that historical moment, combined with the pain felt by others. I was in misery.

Quickly I came to understand two very important concepts. First, I learned that I alone am responsible for my actions. During my life's review, I could not blame others for what I had done. Each of us decides his or her actions, even if you had been horribly abused, as I was, there was no excuse for treating others the same way.

The second thing I learned is that our thoughts, words and actions are extremely powerful and have an effect upon more people than we know, like the far-reaching ripples in a pond after a rock is thrown into it. The effects of our actions touch people that we are not even aware of. But unlike the ripples in a pond, the ripples or effects of our life's actions also come back to us, for good or for bad. If we had good thoughts and actions that helped and lifted others, we will feel the benefit as they ripple back to us. Unfortunately, the opposite is also true. Acts of unkindness and cruelty will have their negative impact upon us as well.

As I watched the actions of my life in review, I became ashamed of many of the things I had done. I began to feel the pain that I had inflicted upon others during the course of my life. To help you understand to some degree, I will relate one small incident. Believe me when I say that there were many things worse than this one episode, but hopefully it will show the pain caused by what I thought at the time was a seemingly insignificant event, and will also help in understanding what I felt at that time.

I had terribly mistreated a girl I knew while living in one of my foster homes. I had long forgotten her and how I had treated her, but now in my life's review it was all there. I remembered every action and every cruelty.

The greatest happiness I had ever experienced was while living in one specific foster home. I was 14 years old at the time. The family was quite well to-do, and had a large home. The father was very kind to me but the mother was cruel. They had a daughter my age named Joanne who was beautiful, kind and talented. When I arrived at their home, I owned two old cotton dresses in very poor condition and a pair of tennis shoes. Joanne and her sisters had closets full of nice clothes that appeared absolutely beautiful to me. Upon my arrival Joanne threw open her closet doors and said, "What is mine is now yours. Wear anything you want." This seemed incredible to me and so different from my past experiences, but I was grateful and began sharing her wardrobe. My new foster sister was very popular at school and church and was always surrounded by lots of friends. Since I was now part of her family (and I still call her my sister), I was included in the popular groups.

There was another girl attending both our school and church that the world would deem unattractive. She was overweight, had dark bushy eyebrows, a ruddy complexion, and some visible facial hair.

You need to understand that I look at people very differently now than I did at that time, before I learned this valuable lesson: Our appearances here on earth are only temporary; everyone's spirit is beautiful. Now I no longer see anyone as unattractive.

Everyone in our popular crowd made fun of that girl, and she was the object of many rude comments and jokes. Though my "sister" and I never said anything to her face, as many others did, and I'm thankful that I was never that cruel, but we were unkind to her behind her back.

We purposely excluded her from almost all of the activities that we were involved in, including the social gatherings at my foster home. In short, we were not very nice to her, and my hypocrisy and lack of kindness came through very loud and clear during my life's review. Here I was a skinny little poor girl. Through the mercy of a kind, religious family, I had been taken in, dressed up and accepted into the "in" group, and my sister and I had shut out another.

I had never before realized how much I hurt this girl by my actions, but during the review, I could feel the pain and heartache she felt as my attitude affected her. There was especially one time, when we snubbed her badly. Suddenly, the pain of this one unkind act was so great for me that I began to understand in a very small degree the agony experienced by many people throughout history who have suffered from cruelty and neglect. It felt as if my spirit body would disintegrate, so great was the pain I felt over this one memory.

To this day, I have been unable to find this girl so I could apologize. I have a small hope that if she reads this book and recognizes her place in my life, she will contact me. The memory in me of the pain that she felt still haunts me, and I hope that someday I can ask her forgiveness in person.

Since my return to mortality, I have attempted to right as many of the wrongs as I possibly could. I have found people that I had harmed in many ways; those I had gossiped or lied about and humbly asked for their forgiveness. Several years ago, I visited a foster mother who had been very mean to me, and I was able to turn that experience around for good. When I went to visit her, in her front room there were family members and friends there with us. I thanked her for allowing me to live in their home and was very grateful that she taught me how to cook healthy foods. Everyone in the room started crying because with her voice shaking, she asked me to forgive her for how she treated me. I walked over and hugged her in her wheelchair and told her I loved her. Hopefully, these steps will erase some of those events from my future life's review.

I still cannot forget what I felt as I watched my review, but I realize that what I felt that day was only a small glimpse of what I would have felt had I passed through the "film" to really go "fully" into the spirit world.

I saw incidents and events in that review that I had totally forgotten. Many seemed so small to my mortal eyes, and they seemed insignificant. Yet, there they were, every detail, good or bad, every part of my life experience on earth.

There are still things in my life left undone, so to speak, which cause me great pain. There are some things I cannot make right with others, and so I have asked the Lord in prayer to please help me and forgive me for those things I cannot undo. The greatest challenge I face is to forgive myself as I remember vividly the details of my life prior to my death experience.

Christ Enters the City

During and after my life's review, which lasted only seconds, I felt terrible and was very shaken. It was only then that I noticed something going on in the distant city that caught my attention. An extremely bright light had seemed to enter and was moving down one of the walkways. This light was so brilliant that it out-shown the light of the city. It was a white light unlike our sun or any other light source I am familiar with. It was so much brighter than anything or anyone else around it. It was then that I realized the source at the center of this light was a man walking. The light emanated from Him, from his body and clothing. His clothes seemed to be made of light. Immediately around His person was a golden glow with beams of golden sparkling light pouring from his body and reaching out a considerable distance. As I looked closer, the sparkling light in the golden beams appeared like fragmented gold dust that was actually a part of the beams.

The man was very beautiful. In an instant I knew that this was Jesus Christ making a visit to the city. He didn't appear at all like the pictures we often see of him. He had no beard and His hair was dark golden blonde. His eyes were as blue as an azure sky, almost unreal. But, like most things in the spirit world, it wasn't His appearance that was so overpowering, it was the feelings and information and everything that was transmitted to me as I looked at Him. He was glorious beyond description even though I was very far away.

As He walked down the streets, people gathered around him in a huge crowd of hundreds and hundreds, yet there was no pushing or shoving. They reverently and courteously came as close to the Savior as they could. Those closest to Him touched His clothes or person, and some embraced Him.

While watching the people, I knew they were feeling His great love for them, which was overpowering. It was so strong that I could also feel it. Those who could not get close enough to touch Jesus could feel His love through the golden beams of light emanating from Him.

I thought to myself that this light must spread throughout the universe and to us on earth as well, so that all people everywhere can feel this tremendous love if they want to. It was as if love was emanating from Him out into the universe, permeating time and space.

As I looked upon the distant scene, only one person in the city looked back at me. He appeared handsome to me, had dark hair and dark eyes, and caught my eye just for a second. When our eyes connected, I understood that he was to be my child. I thought, "That cannot be. I am not supposed to have any more children because of my diabetes." The thought lasted for just a moment. The fulfillment of this encounter came much later.

I Am Greeted by A Beautiful Woman

At that moment, I wanted nothing more than to go down into the city. I do not know if my intent was to ask His forgiveness through my tears or merely to embrace Him and bask in His love. I needed so desperately at that moment to feel His forgiveness and love in the despondent aftermath of my life review. Before I was able to begin movement toward the city, however, I could see a beautiful woman coming up behind me, along a path.

I recognized powerfully at this time that I could see with every part of my body, not just my eyes, so I was aware of what was happening all around me. I could even see out of my fingertips. It was strange and wonderful to have that spirit body, a creation of light and substance beyond earthly description and capable of doing so much more than our bodies of flesh.

As this beautiful woman approached nearer, I turned around to face her. Her hair was a darker blond and swirled up on her head in what we call a French twist. She was wearing a pastel peach colored robe with a turquoise cummerbund around her waist, a cream colored over-the-shoulder sash down to the ground, and she was barefoot. Her robe had a soft glimmering sheerness to it that seemed to flow like liquid and yet it was opaque.

I did not recognize her, though she seemed somewhat familiar. It seemed that I should know her, but I had no idea who she was. As I looked at her, I was somehow able to determine that she was an older woman, even though she looked to be about 30 years old. Another wonderful thing about the spirits I saw is that they all looked to be somewhere in their twenties or thirties. They were all absolutely beautiful and perfect and while I could easily tell them apart from their individual distinctive features, I was also able to recognize them by "reading" their light.

Upon reaching me she said with surprise, "La Nelle, what are you doing here?" I questioned what she meant and how she knew my name. I understood intuitively that there was some kind of signal that alerts family members in the spirit world when a relative on earth is about to cross over. This provides the opportunity for them to be there and dress the new arrival, sometimes even before they leave the body. This woman, whom I did not know at the time, a few years later I discovered was a relative of mine. She had been caught by surprise, somehow knowing that it wasn't my time to die or "cross over." So, she had hurried to reach me.

I tried to grasp the thought that it wasn't my time to die and more understanding began to flood into my thoughts. Apparently, all of us have an allotted length of time to spend on the earth. No righteous person in this world dies before his or her time. So, when a beautiful little child dies, or a beloved grandma or grandpa, or a sixteen-year-old nephew or sweet neighbor, we should not be overly concerned. If they had lived a good life, their death is correct according to God's plan, even though it may be a time of sadness to those left behind. Sometimes a person's time can be cut short by use of drugs, alcohol, tobacco, or other poor choices of how they care for their body, and they lose the benefit of that time on earth. But, as I perceived it, the timing is more important than the way or manner a person dies.

I also understood that we have the choice or option to shorten our allotted time. I had tried to do so by committing suicide, but there would be consequences. This was a wrong choice to make. I thought about my death and immediately realized that for many suicides there is a great penalty or price that has to be paid. Later in Spirit Prison, I would learn that there are different kinds of suicides, and each is judged differently. There are those who are not in control of their minds at the time of their suicide. Judgement for them would be less than others who kill themselves perhaps so they will not have to pay for some terrible crime they have committed, like when a person takes the life of another, then takes their own life.

Jesus knows and understands all of the circumstances present that cause a person to take such a drastic measure, even though to commit suicide for any reason is the wrong choice. He takes all of that into consideration in a way no one else can when making decisions in these situations. Our "assignments" in the Spirit World are determined by the choices we have made and how we have lived our lives while in mortality.

This entire chain of thoughts passed through my mind in the time it took this beautiful spirit woman to hesitate between words. She continued, "You cannot stay here. You have to go back." Hearing this, I started to cry because I had planned to go down to the city and wanted with all my heart to see the Savior and ease the pain I was feeling. I protested, "I don't want to go back. I don't want to go back."

Just then I felt something pulling at me like a huge vacuum cleaner sucking me into a different area. Before I could say or do anything else I found myself in a separate spiritual realm, the place many refer to as hell. I called it "Spirit Prison."

CHAPTER 3

I Visit "Hell"

A Terrible Place, Darkness and Despair

Though I saw wondrous things and experienced the amazing abilities of the spirit body while in "Paradise," the most singular, life changing event in this experience was in the place called "Hell" by we as mortals.

Total Darkness

In a moment, I again changed locations. This time I was transported to a place of near-total darkness with subtle shades of gray and black. Several things hit me all at once, and the total impact was almost ferocious in intensity. All of my newly discovered senses were bombarded simultaneously with fear and heavy darkness. The total effect is hard to describe because it was so overwhelming.

I had been in a place of extremely bright, penetrating light, but now found myself surrounded by almost complete darkness.

But it was much worse than mere darkness. It was a heavy and oppressive blackness. I could feel it pressing upon my spirit body.

Overwhelming Sounds

The sounds around me were also felt with my whole being rather than just heard with my ears. They were awful and pierced into me, filling me with a sense of fear and dread. At first, I thought the sounds were from tortured animals wailing in pain, but I quickly realized almost in horror that these unbelievable sounds were coming from people. Many were weeping. Others were sobbing hysterically. Still others were wailing and crying in terrible anguish, not caused by physical pain, but from unbearable inner torment.

Around that same time, I also became aware of things moving in the blackness. If I focused, I could make out the silhouettes of people, the very same people who were making the pitiful, mournful and almost inhuman sounds.

As I moved about, I could actually feel an intense pressure surrounding my body, relentlessly pressing against me. I started to feel claustrophobic, like drowning in thick goo. It came into my mind that the "air" I felt, was some tangible substance that locked the spirits into this dark place and did not allow them to cross over into the beautiful light part of the spirit world. The thick goo was similar or related to the "screen film" I had observed twice in the place of beauty, but different in its function.

As I slowly moved around in this awful place, surrounded by the darkness, I felt the cries of these tormented spirits with all of my senses. It caused me to ask in my mind, "Am I here because I took my life?"

My Questions Are Answered

The answer came quickly, "No." I believe this is because I was clinically depressed at the time of my suicide. This was a place of temporary confinement for the spirits who had committed acts of evil in their lives on earth and, having not repented of them, had to suffer for their choices. They were suffering a penalty for

71

their sins that would help them understand the broad consequences of evil. People in the mortal sphere refer to this place as "Hell" because it is so very horrifying. Here in the spirit realm, they called it "Spirit Prison." Hell is in a separate realm.

I understood that there were several parts to this spirit prison. I was in the smallest and worst part of this dark place of sorrow. However, I was impressed with the thought that the entire area was huge, perhaps even larger than the light-filled beautiful, peaceful part of the spirit world.

People who had committed heinous, horrible crimes against their fellow men were confined in this terrible place. Here they would feel the pain they had inflicted upon others, but enormously multiplied for a period of "time." They were in agony beyond mortal words or comprehension.

I also understood that many spirits held here were still filled with the same hate and anger that had consumed them while upon the earth. I was permitted to feel a small part of their emotions - the desires to murder, inflict pain, and destroy - that they had felt in their mortal lives. These desires had remained with them after death. While in the Spirit Prison, they continued to attack each other, but a spirit body cannot be hurt.

I asked the question, "How could a loving God put any of His children in a place so terrible and dark?" The answer came immediately to my mind, "God did not put them here. Their own evil deeds drew them there." I then understood that their actions and desires while on earth drew them to this terrible place and the darkness of their thoughts would not allow them to leave to the realm of light. I didn't exactly understand how it worked, but the answer satisfied me.

There Is No Light Here

I also understood that the reason it was so dark was because the people who were here had no light within them. I then was given to understand that in the part of the spirit world I had just left, everything was so bright because everything had light coming from it. The plants, the animals, the buildings and especially the people all had light coming from their bodies. That is why they didn't need to have a sun or a star to give them light. They all produced their own light. I then remembered that I had not seen a sun in the sky, but that everything had been so bright as if it had been in the middle of the day. Here in this place, everything was so dark because the people here were dark. They had rejected the light and turned against it, and therefore it wasn't in or part of them.

While listening to the cries of these people and feeling their pain, something very strange came over me. I began to feel very badly for them. It was strange to me because I had never felt sympathy for anyone back on Earth. My attitude had always been that it was a dog-eat-dog world. I was going to take care of myself and let everyone else get along the best they could. But here I was feeling sincere pain and concern for those around me.

I wondered how long they would have to stay in this dark place. I instantly knew that some of them had already been there for a very long time, over a thousand years as time is measured on earth. Many others would stay perhaps for another thousand years or until they had fully repented of the things they had done. But at the same time, I knew it was more than just repenting. They were paying a price, the consequences for their actions, in some sort of cosmic, spiritual way I could not completely comprehend.

I was extremely frightened as I asked my next question. "Am I going to have to stay here for the things I have done?" I was terrified at the thought of staying in this awful place filled with such great pain and sorrow. I knew that I could not stand to be here for two minutes, let alone a thousand years. I began to feel tremendous pain. I was not ready to weep with these people.

I cried in my heart, "I cannot stay here!"

"Is this where I am going to be for a thousand years? Must I stay in this place until I have paid the price for the actions and choices of my life?"

I Stand Next to My Father

At that exact moment I felt my father standing next to me. I did not turn to look at him, but I could feel his presence. There was no doubt in my mind that it was my father.

Suddenly, I was able to feel a small part of the pain that he was feeling for the life he had lived. It was so completely overwhelming and excruciating that even twenty-two years after that experience I could still feel the pain my father felt and hear him crying.

I could not bear to look at him. As I stood there hearing him cry and feeling his horrific pain, the spirit of hate that caused me to hate him and everyone else, that had been my constant companion during life, suddenly and inexplicably left me in an instant.

Previously, it had been as if I had carried a drawn sword in my hand and used it often to cut down everything and everyone in my life. This experience with my father, and the other spirits in this part of spirit prison took the sword out of my hand.

I felt so sorry and so badly for him that I just wanted to put my arms around him, perhaps to give him some comfort, but I was not allowed to touch him.

I just stood there feeling his pain and the change that had taken place in his heart from the life he had lived. I realized that there had been a change in his heart from when I had known him. Now he had real sorrow for the pain he had inflicted on others.

I realized that he was repenting, but it was so excruciatingly painful and slow and it would take a very long time. Once again, I realized that not only do we feel the pain of what we have done in our own lives, but we also feel the pain that we have inflicted upon others from their perspective. Whatever we have done, we will feel the pain that we caused others to feel if we don't repent here in mortality. This was the source of the unspeakable pain felt by those spirits that caused them to wail like animals.

Next, the thought came to me, "I will be returning to mortality." In that moment, the idea of going back into my "clay body" and to the miserable life I had led, sounded wonderful. Anything to get me out of this place of pain and darkness. Even the trials of life were better than being there.

CHAPTER 4

I See the Future

"I See Many Events That Will Soon Happen in the World"

As I tried to look away from my black surroundings, a small light started to shine in front of me, and the darkness, the sounds, and the feelings that had so completely oppressed me started to fade into the background. The light grew bigger, and a window opened up much the same as when I had witnessed my life's review. This time, however, a panoramic view of the entire earth lay before me. It came closer and closer, or I was getting closer to it, as if I had been out in space flying toward it.

I knew I was viewing these things to help me make my decision about going back to earth and back to my previous life. Part of me wanted to go back to the beautiful part of the spirit world I knew as paradise. Another part of me felt the need to be reunited with my body so I could change my life. It was a tug-of-war, and what I was about to see was to help me understand what I would be going through if I chose to go back into my body.

The view before me played out again like a video recording in fast-forward motion, and yet I could see each scene in perfect clarity. I was able to comprehend everything that transpired.

As I zoomed closer and closer to the earth, I first saw the whole world and then the various continents and countries. It was

76

made clear to me that in the future there would be wars and troubles, including nuclear attacks in various places in the world. I saw a view of how it would start.

Israel Is Attacked, a World War Begins

I had not really studied or known much about the geography of the world, but as I looked at the various lands before me, I instinctively knew which countries they were.

Looking at the Middle East, I watched as a missile flew from Libya and hit Israel. The mushroom cloud that resulted from the blast was visible. I knew that this missile contained a nuclear warhead. I was aware that those who supplied the missile were Iranian, but the missile had been hidden and fired from within the borders of Libya.

Almost immediately after this, other missiles began flying from one country to another, quickly spreading war around the world. I also saw that many nuclear explosions did not come from missiles but from bombs concealed on the ground. Some of them were hidden in large metal suitcases.

My focus then changed from the Middle East to the United States, and I understood that I was about to see the horror that would lead not only to nuclear strikes, but also to many other devastating events.

*Tall Buildings in New York Fall

*Before you read this section, please remember that my near-death experience happened in 1979.

I was interviewed on Fox News and several radio programs, and also gave numerous lectures in which I mentioned this event. At the International Near Death Studies talk, I related the fall of some tall buildings in New York. This was recorded in 1999.

As I looked upon the continent of North America, I focused in on the east coast and then on New York specifically. I saw New York City with all of its people and buildings. Suddenly I saw some tall buildings crashing to the earth. They collapsed like pancakes. They came down surrounded by tremendous amounts of fire, smoke, debris falling like confetti, and thousands of people running and screaming.

As I looked closer so I could see into the smoke and dust. I saw a woman holding a little girl's hand and running from the crashing buildings. The woman had long dark hair, hanging past her shoulders that curled inward slightly. She wore a beige business suit, heels of a slightly darker color, perhaps tan, and she was not wearing glasses. The little girl appeared to be 6 or 7 years old with short brown hair reaching below the chin and cut in a type of a pageboy look.

They ran together, holding hands and trying to escape from the falling buildings. As they ran through the heavy smoke and dust they were forced to let go of each other's hands and became separated.

The child was terrified, and I could hear her screaming, "Mommy, mommy!" over and over again. I don't know their outcome, if they lived or died, but I can still see the face of the woman clearly and could easily identify her from a photo or describe her to a sketch artist.

I asked if an earthquake had caused the buildings to fall. I felt a strong impression and knew in my heart that the answer was no. However, I was not given any indication as to the cause of the destruction.

Around 1992, I told a close friend named Linda P. about seeing tall buildings in New York collapsing, and shared many of the future events I had been shown. On September 11, 2001, Linda P. called me and told me, "Turn on the TV. I saw those towers you told me about." I watched the World Trade Center towers collapse on television, and knew this was what I witnessed years ago. It was like watching a movie I had already seen.

Robot Warriors

Wars and battles were taking place throughout the world. Though many were violent and devastating, the strangest attack on humans I witnessed was an army that appeared to be fierce warriors. They all looked alike, marching in perfect unison.

Even while being fired upon, they did not stop moving forward. It didn't look like they experienced much harm. It appeared to me that there might not be any way to stop them.

These unusual soldiers had the capability of shooting fire from their eyes and fingertips. They could project extremely high-pitched frequencies, inaudible to the human ear yet capable of scrambling the brain of their enemies.

A few of them would open their mouths in the shape of a tall rectangle as they approached their opponents and a vapor of poisonous gas spewed out as an attack on several people. These soldiers also ventured out individually dressed in civilian clothing. Using the same capabilities, they entered planes, train stations, and public arenas.

After closer inspection, and being given a greater understanding, I realized that these soldiers appeared to be man-made robots. They appeared so lifelike with their facial features and body motions, that unless you touched them or paid close attention, you could not distinguish the difference between them and a real human being. After seeing these soulless creatures, I did not want to see any more.

All Commerce Will Cease

I strongly encourage everyone who reads this to have a minimum of a year's supply of food and water for each member of their family. Freeze dried food would be the best. Water will also be necessary because the time will come when all water will be poisoned and undrinkable. During the famine I saw people digging in the ground to look for worms to eat.

Attack with Disease

I saw a man walk into the middle of a crowd of people in the New York Subway and drop what seemed to be a quart jar full of liquid. The jar broke and the liquid spread. People nearby had become infected with a disease from the liquid, and they didn't even know it. A few days later, people became sick and started dying. I saw that similar attacks would happen in many cities throughout the country. I understood that this was a biological weapon. The symptoms included a high fever, vomiting, diarrhea, inability to process food, and eventual death by dehydration. It mimicked a deadly flu.

Another disease started with white blisters, some the size of a dime, appearing on the hands, arms and face of the victims. The blisters quickly developed into puffy white sores. Those with the disease would stumble around and fall over dead. Many died within a short period of time.

Still others were infected with a disease more horrible than the first two. The victims had blood coming from their nose, mouth, eyes and ears. Those with this hemorrhagic disease would melt into the appearance a mass of bloody flesh. These diseases became wide spread across the country with hundreds of thousands infected.

I saw masses of people dressed in shabby clothing, mostly women and children, wandering aimlessly, desperate to get out of the cities. Gangs roamed the streets looting, burning buildings, and murdering anyone left behind. Many people seemed to go crazy. I sensed that the electricity had failed everywhere and that nothing was running throughout the country, including all communications systems. I watched people throw rocks through windows to steal TV's that would no longer work and thought it very strange.

While I watched this all happening in the United States, my view instantly jumped back to the Middle East, and I saw the same thing taking place in Israel. The same sores and the same types of sickness and disease that were plaguing the U.S. had also been unleashed in Israel.

What I saw about the disease in Israel lasted only an instant, then I was back to the United States. There was a tremendously long winter following the siege of sickness. It caught everyone by surprise. The winter started in late summer and lasted into the summer months the following year.

A famine in North America had begun over the few years leading up to the long winter because of storms, droughts, floods and other plagues that had taken place. The abnormally long cold period seemed to suddenly push the famine to its full measure.

After the disease and the long winter, things started going downhill very quickly. Events piled up one on top of another without any breaks. My sense of timing about these events was not very clear because I saw several things happening all at the same time or in very close chronological proximity.

During and after the long winter the disease spread everywhere and increased in severity. The economy and the electricity were completely gone. Without any government there was a total breakdown of civilization. I saw people panicking everywhere. They were trying in vain to find food, but there was none. Chaos and anarchy reigned over the entire United States. There was not one state or city in the country that was not in great commotion. The government had collapsed on every level. There were some local groups, some led by ecclesiastical leaders, who tried to maintain some semblance of order, but as time passed it became increasingly difficult because it was so hard to find food and water and the gangs and marauders had become so numerous and violent that people had to hide in the rocks and caves, or wherever they could. The police and the military were not a factor, having been forced to leave to take care of their own families.

Seeing state by state this disorder and chaos, California was the hardest hit. I saw hundreds of thousands of cars piled up on the freeways trying to get out. Many left their cars trying to walk, but because of the widespread gang activity, the gangs killed many of those who tried to flee California on foot.

It seemed that some of the people had lost their minds and went around in these gangs killing people just for the sake of killing. Many of these were people who had lost access to their psychiatric prescription medications or street drugs. Others killed for food or to rob their victims.

Those who were killing for no reason were like beasts. They were like animals completely out of control as they raped, looted, burned and butchered people. I saw these gangs go into the homes of those who were hiding. They would drag them out of their hiding places, then rape and dismember them.

For many there was an unnatural fear and hatred that came over and clouded the thinking of the people. Family ties that once existed between husbands and wives, parents and children no longer mattered. The only thing that mattered was individual survival. Men would kill their wives and children for food or water. Mothers would kill their children. For me, the events I was seeing were horrible beyond description and unbearable to watch.

Deadly Water

I became aware that there was very little water for drinking. As people roamed from city to city, I understood that much of the water had become contaminated. I did not know if it was disease or nuclear fallout or something else, but all the surface water was now poisoned. Because of their great thirst many people drank the water in spite of the danger of poisoning and died.

While all this was occurring, the people also had to deal with massive earthquakes, tidal waves, volcanoes, oceans leaping inland beyond their bounds, and what looked like stars falling from the sky.

One event I remember specifically seeing was caused by a huge volcano on an island in the Atlantic Ocean. The north half of the island slid into the ocean, causing a massive tidal wave to hit the east coast of North America. The word came into my mind, "Monserrat."

Cities of Light & Safety

The air everywhere seemed to be filled with smoke as many buildings and cities burned. There was no attempt to control the fires. As I looked upon this scene of chaos, smoke, and destruction, I noticed that there were small pockets of light scattered over the United States.

There were, from my best estimation, about twenty or thirty pockets of light. I noticed that most of the locations of light were in the Western part of the United States with only three or four of them being in the East.

These areas of light seemed to shine brightly through the darkness and were such a contrast to the rest of the scene. They quickly caught my full attention. I focused on them for a moment and asked, "What is this light?"

Because of my question I was able to see that these points of light were people who had gathered together and were kneeling in prayer. The light was actually coming from the people, and I understood that the light was showing their goodness and love.

I was given to understand that they had gathered together for safety and that, contrary to what I had witnessed elsewhere, they cared more for each other than for themselves. Some of the groups were small with only a hundred people or so, but other groups consisted of what seemed to be thousands.

I realized that many, if not all, of these places of light, or cities of light as I began to think of them, had somehow been established just before the biological attack and that they were very organized. It was as if they had known what was coming and had prepared for it. I did not see who or what had organized them. I did see many people struggling to reach the gatherings of light with nothing but what they could carry.

These cities of light had food that others outside of those groups did not have. Within the cities of light, the food was readily shared with those who joined their groups. In these places there was peace and safety. The inhabitants were living in tents of all kinds, many of which were no more than blankets held up by poles.

I noticed that the gangs made no threats on these groups and left them completely alone. Many of the people in these cities had guns that they could use for self-defense. The gangs chose to pick on easier targets and unprotected people. They also preyed upon the people who were traveling while trying to reach the cities of light.

As I looked upon the cities of light, I realized that they were temporary. In a short time, the people living within them would go to another place. I did not know where they were going to go, but it seemed that they would gather in the mountains.

The Nuclear Attack on The U.S.

As I was viewing the cities of light, my focus changed, and I became aware of missiles being launched and hitting U.S. cities. I watched as mushroom clouds started forming over many areas of the United States. Some of the clouds came from missiles that I knew were fired from Russia, and others were not from missiles at all, but from bombs that were already within the United States. These latter bombs had been hidden in trucks and in cars driven to certain locations and then detonated.

I specifically saw Los Angeles, Las Vegas and New York City hit with bombs. New York City was hit with a missile, but I think that Los Angeles was hit by at least one truck bomb, if not several, because I did not see any missile. I also saw a huge explosion north of Salt Lake City but without the aid of a missile. This last attack was part of a biological attack on the city.

In the darkness, I also saw fireballs falling throughout the entire country. I'm not sure if this happened just before or during the mushroom clouds. The balls that fell from the sky were of different sizes, most being the size of golf balls, and were very hot. There were millions of them. As they rained from the sky, they left streaks of flame and smoke behind them. Everything they touched caught fire: people, buildings, trees or grass. Everything burned. I didn't ask what the fireballs were or where they came from because by this time I was sickened by the scene before me. I simply observed without asking many questions.

North America Invaded

At almost the same time and in the same locations as the mushroom clouds, I saw Russian and Chinese troops invading the United States. The Russians were parachuting in many spots along the Eastern Coast; I also saw them parachuting into Utah.

Chinese troops were invading from the West Coast near Los Angeles. They met with civilian resistance from those who had survived the disease and bombs. I did not see any United States military there at that time.

This invasion was part of the nuclear war that I had seen earlier. I knew that similar events were taking place all over the world as I had seen previously. I did not see much of this war but was impressed that it was short in duration and that the Russian and Chinese armies were driven back and retreated. I don't have any explanation about how or why I saw these events.

The Earth Cleanses Itself

Now the smoke became very heavy, dark and thick. Just when it appeared things were as bad as they could get, the earth began to shake. This earthquake occurred during the winter, seemingly the winter that followed the very long one I had seen earlier.

The chaos had existed for almost a full year by this time. The earthquakes began in the west, around Idaho and Wyoming, and then quickly spread in every direction. I saw a huge earthquake hit California, which then triggered the faults in Utah. There were earthquakes all over California, but they were especially devastating in the Los Angeles and San Francisco areas. San Francisco is on a shelf that hangs out over the ocean. When the quake hit, it appeared San Francisco turned upside down and fell into the sea.

These multiple earthquakes triggered volcanoes all over the West, and they started spewing a tremendous amount of ash and smoke into the air causing it to become very dark and dirty and blocking much of what was left of the sunlight. I witnessed huge waves of water sweep over the West Coast. This same event was happening to coastal cities all over the world. The waves were so big that Los Angeles was nearly swept away.

In Salt Lake City there was a wall of water perhaps fifteen to twenty feet high that swept through the city. I thought this strange because Utah is so far from the ocean. I had the impression that the wave had not originated at the ocean but came from under the ground. I quickly noticed great cracks or fissures in the earth open up and then saw a great deal of water shooting up out of the ground. I learned that deep under the ground there was a huge amount of water and the earthquakes had forced it up to the surface. The earthquake had already destroyed most of the buildings made of brick, and the glass had shattered in all the new glass and steel buildings, but the devastation was made worse when the water swept over the city. Devastation from water coming up from the ground stretched from Idaho down to near Cedar City, Utah.

Cities all over the country were lying in ruins, and there was rubble everywhere. Most of the buildings were destroyed. However, I realized that even though there was tremendous destruction from earthquakes, disease, floods, volcanoes, and tidal waves, the majority of deaths were caused by the gangs of roving marauders that killed for pleasure.

As I studied this scene for a moment, the thought came to me that this was because the earth itself had become sickened at the terrible acts of cruelty that were happening upon it. The earth itself was causing these natural disasters. It came to me that the earth was attempting to cleanse itself of the chaos and evil that had engulfed the people.

The ash and smoke from the volcanoes had increased, and there was now almost complete darkness everywhere upon the earth. The diseases also increased in devastation, and I saw people literally dying on their feet.

After this second terrible winter, I saw the survivors piling the dead into huge piles to burn them. The stench was sickening. Some of the bodies had been burned during the time of chaos, but because people were more concerned with their own survival, they had mostly ignored the dead around them.

There was a huge earthquake that occurred in the middle of the United States. It was tremendous in size and intensity. It seemed to split the United States in half about where the Mississippi River is. The crack in the earth was miles wide. As it opened up, the earth seemed to swallow everything. Water flowed in from the Gulf of Mexico all the way up to the Great Lakes. The Great Lakes no longer existed because they became part of a large inland sea.

Another series of tremendous shakings began all over the world. These were not separate quakes. Instead, it was one gigantic earthquake that shook the entire earth. The oceans swept beyond their bounds. Huge walls of water engulfed every coastline. The oceans were bright red and smelled terrible because all the fish had died. This earthquake and the walls of water made the earlier ones seem small by comparison.

A mighty wind came upon the earth. As the wind blew violently, people were going into caves and into the cracks of the rocks to try to escape its fury. It appeared to be stronger than any hurricane or tornado. It seemed that everything that had been left was now blown away.

I understood without asking that the great worldwide earthquake and the mighty wind were caused by a huge planet-like object that had come very close to the earth and had disrupted everything. It was also made clear to me that it was very near the end of life as we know it when this happened.

Now my perspective changed. I once again viewed our world from a distance. I saw a huge fireball speeding toward the earth. I felt there was a difference between this event and all the others that had occurred previously, so I asked what it meant. I was impressed that this was the burning of the earth as described in the Bible. I understood that just before the fireball struck the earth, Jesus had appeared. His followers whom I had seen earlier had left with Him and were no longer upon the earth. The few people left behind were the wicked who had somehow survived the earlier devastations. The picture of the earth engulfed by the huge fireball slowly faded away into blackness.

I thought, "I have to return to prepare my children so that they can be protected from these terrible calamities." Apparently, that was the answer to my question whether I should stay in the world of spirits, or if I should return to earth life.

Between the time I answered the question, and before I re-entered my mortal body in the hospital, I saw a vision of Christ on the cross. He spoke to me, mind to mind, and told me, "I did this for you, so you could begin a new life." I felt a strong determination to become a different person. At that time, all the enmity, hate and inability to care about other people completely left me.

I promised the Savior, that very hour, that I would never hurt or be unkind to another human being. Since that day I have tried with all my might to keep that commitment. The Savior has become an integral part of my life. I have tried to serve the Lord in many different ways. I have spent hours on the phone counseling people who have asked me for help. At times, when people are preparing to cross over, I tell them about all of the wonderful things they are going to see and experience. Often times when I have visited individuals in hospitals, they say, "I can't wait to be there." They are no longer afraid of death.

CHAPTER 5

ॐ

My Return to Mortality

The Hospital

As I realized that I was back in my body, just for a moment or two I could still hear the faint cries of the people in spirit prison. Then that faded as well. All of a sudden, I could hear the sounds of a hospital emergency room and feel someone forcing a thick, gooey, awful-tasting liquid down my throat. I then started throwing up again and again. So began my return to mortality.

I was in turmoil while in the hospital. I was groggy, very tired, and wanted to be left alone so I could sleep. Yet, at the same time I didn't want to sleep for fear I would forget what I had seen and experienced. Sleep won out most of the time, but happily I soon realized that I would not forget, so I stopped worrying about it. I constantly thought about my experience during the short times I was awake, but I didn't dare tell anyone at the hospital about it.

I was in the hospital for a couple of days, but no one came to visit me. I was very tired and lonely and I desperately wanted to go home. I kept thinking how wonderful it would be to see my children, and worried that there was no one at the apartment to feed my cat, which I dearly loved.

Two Weeks in an Earthly "Purgatory"

Two very nice policemen arrived one day without warning and took me away from the hospital in their police vehicle. I thought I was going home. Instead, they took me to a psychiatric facility in Hawthorne for an "evaluation" required by state law in cases involving suicide.

Almost immediately after I was admitted, some men in white coats literally dragged a young girl in, screaming at the top of her lungs. They locked her in a room and went away. That set the tone for my entire hospital stay.

I was "incarcerated" with drug addicts, drunks, runaways, and a few mentally disturbed people, both men and women. It was not a pleasant place to be. I spent two weeks there, and I hated every single minute of it. There was no privacy at all, and I really mean no privacy. We were always being watched, even when we took a shower or went to the bathroom. They were always asking stupid questions, often the same ones over and over again. I felt that they were just playing games with me, and I think many of the others did as well.

I soon learned that if I wanted to be released, I should only tell them what they wanted to know. I kept the information regarding my incredible and wonderful experience to myself. It was so bad in there that I tried to lie to them so I could get out sooner. I said I hadn't committed suicide, but rather had been very stressed and took some medication to sleep. I don't think I fooled them. I told the lady psychiatrist questioning me that if I hadn't wanted to commit suicide before arriving at her facility, I definitely would consider it after being in there.

What helped me keep my sanity in the facility was that I remembered everything about my experience. After I returned, people who knew me for years said that they thought an alien pod must have taken over my body to cause such a complete change in my personality. I know that to some this may seem surreal, but no dream or drug-induced experience could have changed my life so drastically. I thought about it constantly. It consumed me. I never wondered if it had been imagined or a dream, I knew without a doubt that it had really happened. The hardest part was deciding what I was going to do about it. The memory of my life review was still fresh. I felt terrible about it and wanted desperately to repent like the man I had seen in the spirit world. I wanted the awful parts of my life to be blocked so they couldn't be read. I didn't know how to begin. After a few months I started functioning again, going to different churches and reading the New Testament daily. That helped a lot.

No friends or family visited or called me while I was undergoing psychiatric evaluation. After two weeks, I was discharged, and my oldest sister, Sandra, came and picked me up in her car. While we drove, she didn't say a word. The silence was deafening. I felt I needed to say something, to help her feel the same change and understanding that I now felt, especially towards my father. I wanted to help relieve the pain I knew she was feeling.

After building up my courage I said, "It is important that you forgive my father for what he did to you. I know what happened." She stared ahead and didn't respond. It was suddenly very cold in the car. I didn't see or talk to my sister after that day, until ten years later.

For a couple of days, I went back to the apartment where I had been living to get my cat and a few possessions. Shaun really didn't care about what had happened to me. He was struggling with his own problems so much that he didn't have time for anything or anyone else. His cocaine addiction was destroying him. I knew I had to get out of there.

I was still tired and confused about what I was going to do in life. I still didn't have a job or any money, and I had no place to live. My experience gave me hope and direction. I knew that I had to make some serious changes in my life, but I still didn't have a clue about how or where to begin. I had a lot of bad attitudes that I had to overcome. The first thing I had to learn was to keep my mouth shut and not say anything negative. For a long time, I didn't say a whole lot. Then I worked on changing my thoughts, even to the point of not thinking bad things about others. I tried hard not to judge people anymore.

I quickly realized that even though I had experienced something truly wonderful, even though I had learned a tremendous number of important and precious truths, my life was not going to be peaches and cream.

I continued working on improving myself and changing my life. I continued reading the New Testament daily, and I took a renewed interest in going to church and studying religions. I went to every denomination I could find – Catholic, Presbyterian, Baptist, Lutheran, Seventh Day Adventist, Buddhist, Jehovah's Witnesses, and a few others. I eventually found a religion that validated what I had learned in the Spirit World about God the Father, His son Jesus Christ, and the true meaning of life.

Sarah (LaNelle)
in the Music Video

I moved into a small garage apartment and was hired at a nice coffee shop in Sherman Oaks called Twains. I made good money there. I never worked at any job I loved as much as I did this one. It wasn't long before I was able to rent my own apartment right around the corner on Valley Heart Drive. My boys moved back home with me. I made some lifelong friends at work – Rick, Katie, and Richard. I worked at Twains for six years.

The Assault and Stabbing

I met an individual at the restaurant. He was pushy and insistent. I told him I was in a relationship, but he kept asking me out every day for two weeks. So, I agreed to go to dinner with him one time. A week later he asked me if I could bring some soup over and sew buttons on his coat. I didn't feel good about it and didn't want to go, but again, he was very insistent. In his apartment, I sat down on the couch and took my sewing kit out. He walked in front of me and without warning hit me in the face so hard it knocked me off the couch. He continued to hit me in the head, asking me questions which I never seemed to answer the way he wanted me to. At one point I ran into the bathroom, locked the door, and screamed for help. He kicked the door in and put a gun to my head. The assault lasted a couple of hours. I begged for my life, saying I had two teenage boys at home who need me, but he kept telling me to shut up. Near the end of the assault, while I was undressed, he stabbed me in the stomach and twisted the knife. He said, "Do you have a baby in there?" I knew he was going to kill me. I yelled out, "In the name of Jesus Christ, leave me alone!" It made him stumble back and that was when I was able to run out of the apartment to my Volkswagen Beetle in the underground parking. I drove home, though I was suffering from a concussion. The wound wasn't too deep, and I recovered fairly quickly. My attacker was arrested and sent to prison for nine years for what he did to me, and the fact that he was running the largest burglary ring in the San Fernando Valley. I found out later, after he was released from prison, he had returned to Twain's and asked the workers there if they knew where I had moved. They didn't tell him anything. When I heard about this, it upset me terribly that he was looking for me.

My new, more positive attitude helped me overcome this horrible experience. I found myself being content with my life, even though it was still difficult.

I Tell My Experience to Frank

Before moving to Utah, while still working at Twains, I first told my full story to someone. One late afternoon an elderly man, who appeared to be in his seventies and down on his luck, came in.

As I went to take his order, I noticed that his hands were shaking really badly, so bad that he was spilling coffee all over the counter. I asked him, "Are you all right?" He started crying right there in front of everyone in the restaurant. I waited for him to gain control of himself for a moment, then he said, "A pretty girl like you would not understand."

I replied, "Yes, I would. I can understand what you're going through."

Gradually, it came out that he didn't want to live any more. He was a former top chef in some of the best restaurants in Los Angeles, but had problems keeping a job because of his drinking.

Because of his problem, he was involved in a terrible car accident one night when he had been drinking. His wife of forty-plus years died in the crash. He could not forgive himself. His life had fallen apart after that, and now he had come to the end of his rope.

He felt that he had failed in life and there was no reason for him to live. Even though he had quit drinking, his situation had not improved. He felt like he was a worthless bum and that he might as well end it all. He didn't know how to do it, but he was going to do it that night.

I told him, "Listen, I really need to tell you something very important, but I can't do it here. Will you promise me that you will not do anything tonight and come and have dinner with me at my apartment tomorrow night? I can then tell you something that can help you. But if you still want to commit suicide after you hear my story, I will not try to stop you."

He hesitated for a minute and then looked me in the eye to see if I was "for real." He then said he would have dinner with me. I gave him my address and phone number. I made him promise again not to do anything until after the next night. He said his name was Frank. The next night we had dinner and I told him about my experience. I started with my life before, and told him about my suicide. I told him my experience in the spirit word. I told him everything. It affected him, and he went home saying he wasn't going to do anything other than just think about what I had told him. I gave him a book containing verses from the New Testament, and he promised to read it.

We talked several times, and he came into the restaurant every day after that. We became good friends and talked often even after I moved out of California. It took him a while, but he started putting his life back together. He even started to take some classes at a community college to improve himself. Eleven years later, I received a phone call from the LA police saying that he had died of a heart attack. They had found my name and phone number in his wallet and so called me. They sent me some of his personal effects, including the book of scriptures I had given him. I know he truly is in a much better place, and I know I will see my friend again.

Adventures at Sybil Brand

Shortly after I met Frank, my son Sean was back living with me, and we decided to move out of the state again. We left our apartment and moved most of our possessions into a storage unit in preparation for the move. I had worked and saved about a thousand dollars for the trip. As Sean and I were leaving town with personal items and the cat in the car, we were stopped by a police officer because he could not see the temporary registration in the back window. It had come loose and was folded over and not visible to him.

When he checked my license, he found that there was a bench warrant out for my arrest. A few years earlier I had received a twenty-dollar traffic citation for not quite stopping at a stop sign. With the confusion and hardships of life, I had put the citation in a kitchen drawer with a bunch of other papers. When preparing to move, I took the drawer of papers and dumped them in a box. I tried to explain the situation we were in, but it made no difference. I was handcuffed and hauled off to the nearest jail. The officer had no sympathy for my situation, or for abandoning a fifteen-year-old boy who didn't have a place to stay, any money, or even a driver's license, on the streets of West L.A.

This happened around 11 a.m. I was transferred to three different jails, and finally booked into Sybil Brand Jail at 2 a.m. the next morning. Sybil Brand is in East L.A. This is a women's facility with one of worst reputations of any jail in the country. I was put in with the worst of the hardened female criminals. These were murderers, prostitutes, and drug dealers. My cellmates were two prostitutes who kept threatening me, saying I would never get out of there alive because they were going to kill me. They finally had to restrain one of them by tying her to a cot with thick leather straps. After a humiliating strip search and other indignities, I felt that those who were in charge of the prisoners at Sybil Brand were just as horrible as many of the people who were incarcerated there.

I was taken to a large room full of women. By this time, I had not eaten and was starting to feel very weak. I desperately needed an insulin shot, but they had taken my purse with my insulin and the money I had saved for the move. Later that morning they brought everyone breakfast. The jail nurse came in the room. She was a crusty, crude woman who had no visible signs of compassion whatsoever and refused to give me insulin.

She ignorantly asked, "How do you know you are diabetic?" I told her that I had been taking insulin for ten years and gave her my doctor's name. She did nothing, and within a short period of time I collapsed unconscious in a diabetic coma.

My cellmates banged on the door to get the attention of the guards. When the guards found me unconscious in my cell, they got the nurse to return. When she found me, she gave me a large injection of glucagon, a highly concentrated sugar solution, which was the exact opposite of what I needed. Any trained nurse would have known that this was a serious mistake. Later I wondered if she had done it intentionally to cover her original medical blunder, as dead men tell no tales. I should have died at that time, but I didn't. I was taken to the jail hospital and remained there drifting in and out of a coma for what I remember being about nine days.

After I improved enough to be transferred from the hospital, I was taken back to a holding cell in the West L.A. jail, where I was originally arrested. There, I waited for a chance to see a judge.

While there, I became weak and shaky and tried to tell the guards that I needed sugar or juice for diabetic shock. I gradually became more desperate and again banged on the door and begged them for help, but they only responded with lewd overtures and crude remarks. I have never heard worse taunting and harassment in my life. They called me a "junkie" and refused any request. It didn't help that I had bruises from the IVs still visible on my arm from my hospital stay while in my diabetic coma.

I went into insulin shock and convulsions and was taken by ambulance back to the jail hospital. It took four or five days to stabilize me after this ordeal, and then I was taken back to the holding cell in West L.A. Eventually I was able to go to court and stand before the Judge. After reviewing my records and hearing my story, he said this whole situation was a travesty and should never have taken place. The prosecuting attorney took me into a small room and told me that I had the makings of a multimillion-dollar lawsuit. "But I didn't tell you that," he said. I was then sent back to Sybil Brand to await my release. I was finally allowed to leave at 1 a.m. in the morning, however I was told I could not wait inside the building. There were a few stone benches in front of the jail, where I waited until morning. This was in East L.A., in a very dangerous part of town. All night I was terribly afraid of what could happen to me.

The crowning injustice was that the thousand dollars I had saved to move out of California was now missing from my purse. I did not dare say anything about it at that point for fear of retribution. As soon as I was free, I started calling friends to get a ride to some place away from the jail and finally found a friend named Dan at home. Dan was willing and able to come and get me. We had become good friends while working on a movie together.

Sarah (LaNelle) in the Movie

The next morning, after some much needed rest, I started calling friends to find Sean. He had been staying with a family we had befriended earlier. After I found him and we were reunited, we spent the next three months living in my Volkswagen Beetle in North Hollywood. Sean slept in the back seat and I slept in the front. The cat was on the passenger side floor. Sean took a bus to school and I worked at Twain's. I gradually saved enough money so that we could fulfill our dream and move out of state. Previous to my incarceration, the manager of Twains, Ida Mae, did not like me. She was afraid that the owner of Twains, Mr.

Clemens, would pursue me. She was jealous of me because she had been in love with him for years. This time however, when I returned to work from being in jail, I had lost ten pounds and was visibly worn out from the experience. When she saw me, her whole attitude changed toward me. She yelled at the cook, "Make her a roast beef sandwich." After that day we became very good friends. She knew Mr. Clemens had taken me to movies and out to dinner, but by this time, she also knew I was a religious girl and he and I were only friends.

I met a young girl named Allison who was visibly pregnant. She came into Twains looking for work. After working there for about a week, the girls told me she was planning to have an abortion. I invited her to come to my apartment so I could talk to her about her plans. I gave Allison every reason why she should not abort her baby, but she would not listen to anything I said to her. A voice came into my mind and I repeated what I heard. I said to Allison, "What if I gave you $10,000 and I adopted your baby?" She thought for a minute and then said, "Okay." I thought to myself, "Where am I going to get $10,000? I just work in a coffee shop."

I know God meant for me to adopt this child. Before the baby was born, I was determined that we would move out of Los Angeles to Utah. I did not want to raise him in Hollywood. Miracle after miracle happened during the remaining six months of when she was carrying her baby. At this time, my sister Deborah sold our mother's house in Orem, Utah, and we each received $2,000 from the sale. I immediately gave that to Allison and told her I would pay her $300 per month towards the adoption. I ate Top Ramen every night for almost a year.

While the adoption was in process, a miracle happened. A man I had never seen before came into the restaurant, and we started talking. He was kind and friendly, and we talked for a while. I told him that I was working as many hours as I could to earn enough money to pay for an adoption of a newborn baby. He

101

said he would like to help in some way. I politely turned him down a couple of times because I didn't want to have any strings attached involving a man.

He came into the restaurant the next day and handed me an envelope, and then left. I was too busy waitressing to look to see what was in it, and tucked it into my apron. At the end of the day, I opened the envelope and found $2,000 and a note saying it was for the baby. I never saw him again. I thanked the Lord profusely for this miracle, as the money was sorely needed.

I always gave Allison her money when I got paid, but one time I was a day late. When I came home there was a note on my apartment door. It was from Allison. It said, "I want the baby back. You are late on your payment."

It was touch and go with the adoption for three years until I was finally able to stand in front of the judge in court with my baby. I named him Elias John Menet, and finally, he was legally mine. The day after the adoption, Elias turned three years old.

Within a week following the adoption, I returned again to Utah with only $50 in my pocket. I stayed in a friend's basement until I could find work. I returned to Linda P.'s large estate in the Provo River Bottoms and she hired me for a second time. I loved working for her. She had seven children and I performed several duties in her home. I made breakfast

Sarah (LaNelle) and Elias (Age 5)

and got them all off to school. I washed several loads of laundry every day. I cooked a gourmet dinner with a homemade dessert every night. I became very fond of her children and I am still close to them to this day. Linda was not only my employer, but we also became very close friends. After 30 years of spending a lot of time together, we now are more like sisters.

When Eli had turned five years old, I moved into a condo in Orem. One morning I woke up with a terrible headache and couldn't see. Everything was blurry, and I couldn't focus on anything farther than about three feet away. I felt terrible all over so I had a friend take me to the hospital. After an examination I was told that I was going blind as a result of years of being a diabetic. They informed me that there was nothing they could do for me and that I would probably go completely blind over the next three or four

Elias (Age 13)

months. However, I made contact with an eye surgeon who wanted to try surgery on my eyes to possibly improve them. He operated on my left eye, but I never returned to do the right eye because for four months after the surgery, every time I blinked it felt like broken glass in my eye and my left eye wept constantly from the pain.

The Swirling Tunnel of Stars

I learned to adjust to having limited sight. Shortly after, I woke up with severe pain in my kidneys. It was so bad that I couldn't even reach the phone to dial 911. My five-year-old son called my close friend, Linda P. so she could take me to the hospital. The pain was so severe that they had to carry me out to the car. I was told that my face was ashen gray, and I had become limp like a dishrag. As we were speeding in the car to the hospital, Linda P. was saying, "Hold on Sarah, you're going to make it." I would reply, "No, I am not. I am going to die this time. I see a tunnel of swirling stars." I knew what that meant. I was never afraid. Then I must have passed out because I don't remember any more.

The hospital was close by, and they rushed me into the emergency room. When I regained consciousness, I was still in a lot of pain. I was told that my kidneys had failed as a result of diabetes. As I recuperated, I was informed that I needed to have a kidney transplant and that I needed to start dialysis very soon. Otherwise, I would probably die within a year or two. I surprised them when I told them, "No, I don't want a kidney transplant or dialysis. I am not afraid of dying, because I know that God will not take me back until it is my time." I did allow them to give me a blood transfusion.

While in the hospital, I asked my doctor if I could visit the terminally ill patients on that floor. She said if I felt strong enough, she would allow it. Dressed in a long white nightgown, and pulling my I.V. bottle on a stand, the first patient I visited was an elderly lady, who said, "Are you an angel?" I asked her if she would like some company. We visited for a while before I found an opening to tell her about the Spirit World. She loved hearing about paradise, and after a long visit she did not want me to leave. She said that she was now very excited to go there. I told her that I would visit her again the next day, but when I returned to her room she was no longer there. I was very grateful that I was able to spend that time with her.

My Life Is Spared for a Purpose

While I was in the hospital recuperating, a minister who was a close friend of mine came to visit and gave me a special blessing. In the blessing, he told me that, "Satan desired to destroy me, but the Lord was going to spare my life so that people would hear my voice."

What he said stunned me. He didn't know anything about my experience and had no way of knowing what it meant to me for him to say that. He told me that he felt strongly that I should begin to share my experience with others. When he left, I thought a lot about what he said. I knew he was right, but I was not sure how to begin.

My doctors said that I made a remarkable recovery and I was sent home after five days. Approximately a week after I arrived home, I had a difficult time breathing. I was struggling for air, and then I collapsed. My five-year-old son, Elias, called 911, an ambulance arrived, and they took me back to the hospital. This time, it was for congestive heart failure. Water from my kidneys had backed up into my lungs and into my heart, causing serious complications. I found myself back in the same hospital ward, only this time I was too tired and exhausted to do much visiting. After being released, it took me nearly a year to regain my strength.

Since that time, I have given multiple lectures throughout Idaho and Utah. I am still legally blind, my kidneys continue to not function properly, and I recently experienced a heart attack. I still contend with other health challenges.

Real Love Finally Came to Me

Nearly every Friday Night, I would attend a church dance with my girlfriends. One night at the dance, a tall, handsome cowboy named Brandon asked me to dance. After we finished dancing, he asked me if I would go on a date with him. I told him, "I don't date." Every Friday night after that, he would approach me and ask me again if I would go out with him. After asking me several times, I was very rude to him. He had a very hurt look on his face and I felt bad that I had been so mean to him. I stopped going to the dances for a while so I wouldn't run into him again. Weeks passed and I saw him in a local market close to my house. I walked up to him and apologized for hurting his feelings. I asked him if he would like my phone number so we could talk. I said, "Do you have a piece of paper and a pen?" He said, "I don't need it, just tell me the number and I'll remember it." We started spending a lot of time together. He actually was a very nice person, and a lot of fun. After seeing each other for a few months, he gave me an engagement ring and asked me to marry him. I was very happy, but soon after, he just disappeared. I couldn't understand what had happened.

His best friend, Chris, whom I had never met, gave me a call. He said he was very sorry for Brandon's disappearance. Chris said, "By the way Brandon had bragged about me, he was shocked that Brandon had just taken off like that." Chris started calling me every night to see if I was okay. Our phone calls sometimes went on until 4:00 a.m. I had still never met him. Finally, I asked Chris if he would like to come over for dinner, because he had been so nice to me. When I opened the door to let him in, I was shocked when I saw him. He was nothing like I had imagined. He was six foot six, beautiful blonde hair to his shoulders, and his

Sarah (LaNelle) and Chris

eyes looked like he was wearing fake blue contacts, but they were his real eyes. He was very shy and reserved. I asked him if he would like to come over again some time to watch a movie with me. We watched "Schindler's List," not exactly a romantic movie. We saw each other every day after that for about three or four months. He finally said, "I think we should get married." I replied, "I think that's a good idea."

When Brandon heard that Chris and I were getting married, Brandon said, "I am ready to marry you now." I told him, "I'm very sorry, but I don't have the same feelings for you any more, I'm in love with Chris." I heard from friends that Brandon was devastated and moved to Montana. Chris and I were married at Nunn's Park, above Provo in the mountains. My sisters and our closest friends attended. It was a very simple, but beautiful ceremony. We were only married for a year and a half, but it was the happiest time in my life. Chris' mother said she had never seen him so happy and doing so well. Chris was the perfect step-father to my adopted son, Elias. They both loved each other very much. One morning Chris was found dead in his recliner. He was eleven years younger than me and had seemed very strong and healthy. His heart had just stopped.

My world had ended and my happiness was cut short. When my son, Elias, walked into the mortuary and saw the only father he had ever known, lying in his casket, he fell to the ground. He could not understand why God had taken him away from us. He desperately wanted to be with Chris in Paradise. It was rough for the two of us for quite some time.

CHAPTER 6

ौ

Lessons I Learned in the Spirit World

My desire to share important concepts that I learned while standing on the hill in paradise is very strong. During that experience I learned so much so quickly that it would be impossible for me to write it all down.

My learning there was not limited to one concept followed by another like here on earth. Instead, I began with one question and progressed to learning what seemed like hundreds of answers all at the same time. I could assimilate and comprehend all the information perfectly.

Though the main learning session lasted only a few moments, it included answers to some of life's most important questions. Learning took place throughout my experience, but the greater lessons came to me on the wooded hill. The purpose of this chapter is to share some of the marvelous truths I learned at that time, even though human language falls short. It would be similar to trying to describe a television to a pioneer from the 1800s.

The Importance of Love

The most important thing I learned was how very much we are loved. God our Father, Jesus Christ, and the angels all love us more than we will ever know. It is just as important to love and care for each other in our individual lives. This knowledge permeated my entire being and I understood it's great importance. I sensed that everything that Heavenly Father and Jesus Christ do for his children is based upon the love they have for us. It was a very specific love and concern that surpassed every other emotion that I have experienced or could imagine.

It was clear that they know each and every one of us by name, personally and individually, and they know us much better than we know ourselves. They know our faults and weaknesses, yet they also are aware of our strengths and capabilities. They know we will make mistakes as a part of our human experience, but they love and sincerely want the very best for each of us.

One of the most important concepts we can learn, and one of the main reasons we come to earth, is to develop the same kind of pure, selfless love for others as God the Father and Jesus have for us. They can bless us in many ways while in mortality, but in order for them to give us the greatest blessings, we must comply with the spiritual laws that have been given to us in the scriptures.

It is also important to understand that some apparent blessings in mortality are not really what they appear to be. We may obtain wealth and ease through many means both good and evil. If our wealth is gained through evil, it will only be temporary, and the consequences will be severe, sooner or later.

After returning from my experience, I began reading the New Testament daily. I had never read the Bible before, but now I had a great desire to do so. I learned that without charity we have nothing. Charity is the pure love of God. Jesus told us the greatest commandment is to love God, and the second, like unto it, is to love one another. People often confuse this "spiritual love" with physical or romantic love. The kind of love that God is trying to teach us goes beyond the physical senses. We are taught the importance of loving our neighbors the way we would have them love us.

We Are All Beautiful

Another significant concept is that we mortals have confused the meaning of true beauty with that of physical beauty. True beauty comes from within.

Everyone is beautiful, unique, and special, no matter what they look like or what clothing they use to cover themselves. Before my experience, I had become very involved in the Hollywood scene, which is based largely on physical beauty, expensive clothes, and most of all, making more money than they could spend in a lifetime. But all of these insignificant desires are just dust in the wind. We often see rich and famous people drinking and drugging themselves to death because none of these material or physical attainments bring true happiness.

Mortal life can be very temporary. In the scheme of eternity, we are really only on the earth for a few minutes. Have you ever looked back and thought to yourself how quickly your life has passed? Spending so much of our lives focusing and concentrating our efforts on the attainment of power, wealth, beauty and material possessions is an unbelievable waste of time. Our focus should be on improving our minds, overcoming our weaknesses, and developing a love and compassion for all mankind. This is the time for self-improvement. Our time here should be spent serving our fellow man. Heaven will be yours when you learn to put the needs of others before your own. Christ said the greatest commandment is to love Him. The second is to love your fellow man. These were the two great commandments He gave us.

We lived for eons of time with God, our father, as His spirit children before being born into mortality. When we leave this mortal existence, we will spend even more time in the Spirit World until the day of judgement. We will then receive all that God has in store for us.

The Importance of Helping Others

I learned that in our growth here, we can't, nor were we ever intended to "go it alone." We also were not intended to go through these experiences just to benefit ourselves.

We are here to travel this life together. We are here to learn and grow from each other, and to teach each other, thereby succeeding together in the end. We are all connected in one way or another and have known each other in a very real way for a very long time. The person we bump into on the street may have been our best friend before coming to this earth life. Without exception, the people living upon the earth now knew and loved each other before being born. We don't remember it because shortly after we were born, a block, or a veil of forgetfulness, was put on a part of our "spiritual DNA" to prevent us from remembering our lives before coming to earth. However, occasionally a small memory will come through, and we will have a vague recognition of people or places. That is why many of us feel like we know someone the first time we meet them. This is why we sometimes immediately "click" with a person. We feel we have known them "forever." It indeed may be the case.

This reality is one of the reasons I feel so sad when I read about the terrible killings and wars, especially between the Arabs and the Jews. But it is the same for anyone else. In their forgetful ignorance, someone could quite possibly be killing their friends, or people they dearly loved before coming to this life.

That is another reason why our life review and complete remembering when we get to the other side is so difficult and painful. Our memory will be restored, and we will realize the pain we inflicted on our brothers, sisters and friends from long ago.

111

We cannot reach heaven alone. As mentioned before, a major part of this life experience is to learn to love and help others. We cannot live like hermits and expect to go to heaven. I once read that Mother Theresa said, "Love is service to others." I think that is exactly right. It is by serving others, helping them become better people, and loving them, that we learn the true principle of love. We grow and progress by doing things for, and giving to, others in need.

Xoi-Coi

I learned a word that is used in the Spirit World for which an equivalent in our language does not exist. The word is "xoi-coi" (pronounced ex-oy-koy). The word describes someone who doesn't do anything while on earth. This kind of person doesn't progress, doesn't help others, or care. In some ways, he or she just takes up space, and they do nothing worthwhile. Unfortunately, I learned there are a lot of spirits who come to earth and become xoi-coi. They do nothing to elevate mankind or contribute to the improvement of the world. Some contributions may be large and some may be small because not everyone has the same power to make a difference. It is important that we all try. Even very small acts of kindness and goodness can make a big difference.

I recently heard a story about a young man who did a simple act of service that saved someone's life. A boy who was considered a "geek" at school had cleared out his locker and was planning to never return. As he was clearing out his locker, he dropped a large pile of books. Another young man, one of the most popular boys at school, was right there when it happened. He helped the "geek" pick up the books and then walked home with him, carrying some of his books. The two young men became friends.

Years later, the boy who had dropped the books was giving a lecture and divulged that he was cleaning out his locker because he was on his way to do something drastic. He had been so completely discouraged that he had planned to commit suicide later that night. He had cleared out his locker so that no one would have to deal with his mess. The kindly help and smile he was given turned his thoughts around.

Why Must Good People Suffer?

I asked, "Why did I have to suffer so much pain during my childhood at the hands of my Father?" The answer was that none of us suffer more in this life than we are able to handle. Every hardship we experience is designed to help us learn and grow. It is all part of the plan that we helped choose before coming here. I learned that God will always provide a way for us to overcome or handle these challenges.

As God plans and prepares good things for us, I also learned that there is an evil spirit we call Satan. With the assistance of other dark like-minded spirits, he orchestrates bad experiences and temptations in our lives. I know that he is a very real spirit person. He led a group of spirits who rebelled or tried to fight against God a long time before we came to earth. This is what is known in the Bible as the "War in Heaven." I cannot begin to express how deceptive and evil these spirits are. What I am saying is that there is no limit to the mayhem, debauchery, destruction and wickedness that Satan and his co-spirits will do or persuade people to do. These evil spirits cause or instigate most of the terrible and evil events that happen here on earth.

God the Father and Christ are always in complete control, but they do allow each of His children and creations the ability to choose good or evil. Satan and his evil cohorts have the ability to influence people by leading them away from God. By their efforts, we are tested to our limits, to determine which path we will choose. Our actions will stand as a witness or testament for or against us at the day of judgement.

If we did not experience suffering, we could never learn to develop compassion. Without pain or difficult trials, we would not be able to understand or appreciate complete joy.

It is very important for us to understand pain and suffering so that we can help comfort and give love to others. This is one of the main reasons we came to earth. I am not completely sure what all of this means, but I do know that as spirit beings before we came to earth, we never experienced physical pain.

It is also important to know that we are not alone in our pain and suffering. When we hurt, God and Jesus know how we are feeling. They understand our pain and can help us through it. Spirit beings can also feel the joy and pain of other spirits.

The balance is different on earth than in the spirit world, but both work together. There is purpose in everything for learning and developing, especially for learning compassion and love.

The evil spirits who never gained a body and never will, have an advantage because their memories have not been blocked the way ours in mortality have been. They remember the thousands of years we lived together. They knew us very well. They know our weaknesses and attempt to use these against us to persuade us to do wrong. They are in torment and suffering because they will never have physical bodies because of their evil actions and rebellion against God. They are constantly working to make mortals as miserable as they are.

Contrary to popular belief, spirits do have some power over a number of physical objects. Good spirits do not abuse this power, and evil spirits are limited in what they are permitted to do. God's power, and the power of the righteous, is always greater than all the powers of darkness.

For the most part, these evil spirits work by suggesting thoughts into our minds. It is very difficult to resist or fight back due to the fact that under normal circumstances we are not able to see the spirits as they exercise their evil works. After they get a person to listen, they can influence them to do terrible acts that cause the greatest pain and suffering possible against mankind. We can combat their influence by choosing the right. God's influence is also always there for us to choose and follow. We should always pray for guidance. This will strengthen us against the influence of darkness.

There are many dark spirits here on earth. They are all around and have the ability to roam where they want to in our world. Always remember, they can only harm us when we give them power by making bad choices and giving in to temptation. There are numerous times when we can actually feel the presence or influence of these evil spirits. They feel victorious when they influence us to feel hate, anger, or to harm another person in any way. If we let ourselves become uncontrollably angry or full of hate, we can be fairly sure of their presence and attempts to influence us.

When I made the decision to end my life, I was being bombarded by dark thoughts about myself. The thoughts I had were that my children would be better off without me, nothing I did ever worked out, and I felt like I failed at everything I tried. Looking back to the time that this happened, I can see that dark spirits were definitely influencing me.

To counter the influence of those evil spirits, there are many good spirits around us who whisper warnings of physical or spiritual danger. They always encourage us to do what is right. In most cases, these good spirits around us are loved ones or family members who have either passed away or who have not yet been born. They love us and are constantly looking over us. They speak peace and bring hope to our hearts. These good spirits, in many cases, communicate with us through dreams which can often reveal a message we need to pay attention to.

Unfortunately, these dark spirits can also use dreams as a means of communication. When you are in an alpha awareness state of sleep, this is when good or bad spirits can influence your thoughts. Many nightmares are caused or influenced by evil spirits. This is one reason why it is extremely important to pray at night and to ask God to keep us safe from evil. If we fail to ask Him for His protection or His help, that help may not be there. God will not force anything upon us. We must be free to choose our actions. Force comes from Satan. God invites and encourages us to choose Him.

Some of the good spirits have been given special powers to prevent the evil spirits from going beyond their bounds. They are also given power to protect us from crossing over before our time. We call these spirits guardian angels.

In 1986, a group of children in Cokeville, Wyoming were held hostage at their elementary school by a madman and his wife. The man had a bomb in the room where he was holding the children. He was planning on blowing up the school and killing all the children. You can see the details in the movie, "The Cokeville Miracle" which can be purchased online.

In summary, the bomb went off, killing his wife. The man was out of the room at the moment. The bomb and all the children and teachers were in a 30' by 32' room. According to experts, everyone in the room should have been killed. None of the children or teachers were harmed. It was a complete miracle that they lived through.

All of the children later told stories of angels who came down from the ceiling to help them. Some were dressed in white, and others appeared to be dressed in normal clothing. The angels told them where to stand and what to do to prepare for the explosion. Later, during the investigation after the event, many of the children recognized the angels as deceased relatives through family photograph albums. This is just one example of how spirits, either family or beloved friends are allowed to help us here in mortality. I believe that angels accompanied those people who jumped or fell from the Twin Towers on September 11, 2001.

We are always given a choice between good and evil. As I said earlier, it is a sometimes-unseen law that has to be obeyed here. That is why evil will be given an opportunity to become very powerful in the near future. It is all part of the balance required to allow us to make choices.

God often works in mysterious ways. Sometimes that simply means he orchestrates events very differently than we think or believe He should. As an example, I like to think of Moses in Egypt. To our mortal minds, it would have been so simple for God to make Moses the Pharaoh, ruler of all Egypt, then Moses could have easily released the children of Israel from slavery. Then again, perhaps if he had been Pharaoh, he could have been prideful and stubborn enough to ignore the command from God to let the children of Israel leave. However, instead of the seemingly simple way, God set up a confrontation between Moses and Pharaoh. It was a tremendous battle between good and evil, with many plagues and destructions. God showed His will so that the people would see the difference between God's way and man's way. This was part of His plan to help the Israelites learn to follow Him and to follow His prophet. It shows the contrast between good and Satan's evil way as shown through Pharaoh. Even with the many miracles they saw, the children of Israel still had a difficult time being obedient.

The Importance of Forgiveness

I learned an important concept when I encountered my father in Spirit Prison. This was the importance of forgiveness.

117

The people in this hell will not be able to leave that terrible place and progress until the people they have harmed forgive them.

It is not enough that they suffer the pain of the hurt they inflicted upon others, or have a change in their hearts so they no longer desire to injure others. They must receive the forgiveness of the people they have either physically or emotionally destroyed.

We need to understand our responsibility to forgive. We are told in the scriptures that God will forgive who he will, but it is required for us to forgive everyone. Our part in the forgiveness process is extremely important. There is a strange bond between people that hurt others and those who have been injured by them. The way to break that connection is for the person who was harmed to forgive the offender. We must forgive those who have injured us emotionally or physically. It helps to free us from that connection and to make ourselves acceptable to God. Without forgiveness, both the person who inflicted the pain and the person who received it will be bound, dragged down in a spiritual sense, and unable to progress.

Deja Vu

Before we came to earth, we all lived together for eons of time as God's spirit children. We grew up in that environment, making everlasting friendships. We learned all that we needed to know to be prepared to enter earth life. I am sure that we were taught how to show love, kindness, and concern for others. When we obtained all the knowledge necessary to make our descent to earth, we were then sent down and born into a mortal body.

As we were given the final choice between coming to earth, or remaining in the Holy City, we were shown some of what our earth life would be like. God showed us small glimpses of our future and gave us a clearer understanding of what we might have to endure. We knew, to a degree, some of the suffering and challenges we could face. Even knowing what our trials might be, we were still excited for the opportunity to come.

We experienced a great war in heaven. Lucifer's plan was to force every spirit to come to earth and have no freedom. We witnessed Lucifer being expelled from that spirit realm, along with those who followed him.

In Father's plan, every spirit would be free to choose for themselves. All of the spirits who came to earth accepted the plan that Christ presented to God our Father. Every person who ever lived, or would live, on the earth chose to follow Christ's plan.

After we were prepared to come to earth, we formed groups and were organized with those individuals we wanted to have as a part of our earthly families. We chose to be with those spirit beings with whom we had formed close relationships. These were friends we loved and from whom we could learn the most.

Our circumstances in mortality obviously would be varied because of the families we would be born into, the time and place we would be born, and so on. All situations were measured and chosen for our long-term good. Nearly all of us chose to come to earth because we understood that the experience as mortals was the only way to progress. God also showed us some of the harmful and unhappy experiences that would occur in our lives. He wanted our decision to be born to be based on a more complete understanding of what lay ahead.

I was shown how terrible and painful my life would be, and I chose to come anyway. As a spirit, I had been taught that the greater the trials, the greater the opportunity for growth and learning would be. Great and painful situations looked like exciting challenges that we would surely be able to overcome. Of course, the actual experiences here on earth seem much harder than it looked on our "preview screen." Seeing a movie where someone is hurt or in pain is very different from actually feeling the pain.

Deja vu can come from our fragmented memories of those preview scenes that were shown to us. It can also come from dreams we have had about an experience before it happens. That is why we sometimes know exactly what someone is going to say, or we have the sense that we have been in this same place before, because we have already seen it.

Reincarnation

Many people believe they have lived on earth previously, perhaps many times. This is a false belief. We are not able to return to mortality multiple times until we "get it right." Everyone ever born has only one chance to fulfill their life's mission on earth. Then they will be able to either continue their progression or be held back.

As I have mentioned, before we came to earth, we had formed close relationships or friendships with each other as spirits. We wanted to continue our friendships and come to earth at the same time so we could experience life together. Occasionally, however, it was not always possible, and a loved one came to earth ahead of us. When this happened, we could at times receive permission to accompany them to earth as a guardian angel. In this way we were able to be with them and assist them throughout their lives. We could also then closely observe the experiences of their mortal lives and gain a better idea of what earth life would be like for us in the future.

I have an example that I often use to help explain how this works. Suppose one of my very closest friends in the spirit world came to earth a hundred years before I did, and I received permission to come and be one of her guardian angels. I was constantly by her side, heard what she heard, witnessed her experiences, and felt what she felt. In a way I was living her life with her. I was present at her birth and saw her as a little girl when she fell out of a tree and broke her arm. I was there with her when she married her sweetheart and watched with her as he went off to war. I was by her side as she nursed him back to health after he had been wounded and watched with love and compassion as years later, she buried him and a baby at the same time.

A hundred years later I am living on the earth having my own experiences and by coincidence one day I am drawn to visit a house in the South, the very house that my dear friend lived in. The house seems familiar to me and I can tell bits and pieces about the lady who lived in the house. I am able to tell about her birth, family, husband and events of her life. I can tell so much that it seems like I might have actually been her, and that I had lived that life before, and now have been remembering in my present life. In actuality, I am only remembering my friend's life events because I had been by her side experiencing them as a spirit. We only get one chance at living in mortality.

There is no such thing as reincarnation. It is the simple remembrance of shared experiences of someone else's life that has been recorded on our spiritual DNA.

Insects and Animals

I did not see any insects in the spirit world. It was my understanding that when they cross over, they go to an entirely different place prepared just for them – a lower world, a sort of spirit world for insects. Most animals are the same. They also go to a place where they can be happy and be with their own kind. The exceptions are those animals that would be happiest living with a person who loves them. We will be able to enjoy the company of our pets that we loved and had stewardship over while we were on the earth.

People Who Are Murdered

I asked a question about people who are murdered and experience so much terrible pain when they die. I wondered what happened to those who suffered before they died. The answer was comforting. Often, especially in the case of children, the spirit leaves the body before much of the pain occurs so that they do not feel it. Somehow, with His infinite love, God has made provisions so that the body will still appear alive, but the spirit of that person does not inhabit the body any longer and is cut off from much of the torment and pain. Those individuals who participate in the shedding of innocent blood will forever suffer a torment far worse than their victim ever did.

The Mentally Handicapped

People who are born mentally or physically handicapped, for example with Downs Syndrome, knew they were going to be born with that challenge and chose to come anyway. Children born with those challenges are very special spirits, already full of tremendous love. They are some of the very best and most noble of God's children. They come to earth primarily to receive a body and help others learn how to love and give service. In reality, it is a great blessing to have one of these children born into your home if they are welcomed and cared for with love and gratitude. They do not have to be tried and tested in ways that we are, and are already received into Heavenly Father's highest kingdom.

Other Abilities of Spirit Bodies

I became aware of many abilities of the spirit body. Spirit bodies have the ability to travel into the past and actually see, hear and experience things that have already happened. They do not, however, have the power to change or influence outcomes. They can only observe. I found that there are many dimensions, and spirits can easily travel between them. The future is like another dimension, and occasionally spirits are permitted to travel there. Spirits are also able to travel to different worlds and planets if they desire, and it all happens at the speed of a thought. I was impressed that the spirit world actually occupies the same space as the earth but in a different dimension. That is why family members who have passed on know much of what is going on in our lives and are concerned with our progress or lack thereof. In reality, they are very near us.

Life on Other Planets

I have been asked several times if I had any information about life on planets other than earth. The answer is that there are many planets in the universe that are inhabited with beings just like us, because they also are made in the image of God, but we need not be concerned with what is going on elsewhere. They are not a threat to us as many suppose, though it is possible that some of them might visit us. Grotesque beings from other worlds that supposedly visit this earth and are seen by humans are actually evil spirits who can take on whatever form they wish in order to confuse and deceive.

Music, Drugs and Alcohol

Music, as many people are already aware, has a powerful effect directly upon the spirit. Music does have the power to influence for good or evil in varying degrees. It has a kind of spirit of its own. It can encourage us to be better people and motivate us to help others, or it can do just the opposite and stimulate us to do evil and turn away from God. Destructive music consisting of sexual lyrics or violent suggestions can and does attract dark spirits and, in a way, gives them more power over us so that we can be influenced easily to do acts of evil. When I became so depressed that I committed suicide, I played music over and over again that had a negative effect upon me and helped surround me with destructive spirits. The music weakened my spiritual stamina, so to speak, and gave the evil around me greater power. I gave in to the depression and listened to their whisperings.

The music flows past the filters of our conscious minds and makes strong suggestions to our subconscious minds. In a sense it is almost a form of hypnotism. Particularly with young people, the wrong kind of music can lead them down the wrong path. The use of prayer, good music, uplifting books, and so forth, can increase our resistance to evil spirits and actually drive them away.

Drugs and Alcohol are some of the most powerful tools of the demons. One of the goals of these unredeemable spirits is to take control of our bodies. This allows them to feel the senses, pleasures and pain that otherwise they cannot.

Before a spirit comes to earth, it cannot feel sensation. Once a spirit has been joined to a physical, mortal body, its senses are much stronger. After death, when the body returns to dust and is buried in the earth, the spirit's senses are much stronger. However, it still misses the physical body. I came to understand that later on, the spirit and a new, glorious body will be joined together. This is called the resurrection. It happens after spending a period of time in the spirit world. It is at this point that a person is assigned to one of the kingdoms of glory that lie beyond this temporary world.

When an evil spirit enters a human physical body, we call it a "possession." It happens much more frequently than we realize. Possessions can be very mild or extend to complete control. All of us have a natural resistance to such a possession so that evil spirits cannot enter us.

However, when we partake of mind-altering drugs and alcohol, this resistance is lowered. It can happen with the first drink. A hole opens up at the crown of the head that actually allows an evil spirit to drop down into us. Once inside, they have a greater power over us and can influence our behavior to a great degree. This is why Satan and his evil cohorts encourage the use of alcohol and drugs. It is also why so many heinous crimes are committed under the influence of these substances. We will be held responsible for the acts we commit while under their influence. We should never take these substances into our bodies and should be careful of our association with those who are controlled by these mind-altering tools. A hard truth is that Satan often works through so-called "friends" to pull us down.

Many people are under the false impression that occasional recreational drug use does not hurt anyone else. In reality hundreds of innocent lives are lost yearly from drug trafficking. Drug enforcement officers and others are murdered for their continued efforts to fight the losing battle against drugs in our country. If the demand for these harmful substances was to cease then so would all of the evil activities associated with them.

Every time an individual buys or uses an illegal drug, somewhere in the world people's lives are being taken to provide it for them. Both the user and seller are responsible in some measure for the deaths of those souls. There is nothing innocent or harmless in the use of marijuana, misused prescription drugs, or any illegal substances.

Spiritualism, Witchcraft and Sorcery

Along with the understanding of how evil spirits had influenced my suicide (empowered by many of the poor choices I had made), I learned that there are people on earth who encourage and help evil spirits turn others away from God and commit evil acts. Spiritualism, witchcraft, sorcery, Ouija Boards, and so on are all ways that encourage and assist evil spirits. People who engage in these types of activities are easily influenced by these sources and may be led to believe they are talking to a loved one. The Lord has always warned people to stay clear of psychics and mediums for these reasons.

People, who "channel" spirits are always taken over or possessed by the wrong kind of spirits, often pretending to be someone's dearly departed relative or friend. They can do this easily because they have seen our lives and know what has happened and what to say to convince unsuspecting victims.

Those evil spirits also enjoy pretending to be higher beings or aliens from other worlds. They will do anything to get people to believe and listen to them. They are willing to tell many truths to lure people away from God and believe in them, slipping in the one lie that will clinch their control at the most vulnerable, critical moment. Those on the other side who need to know, and have power to help us, are already aware of our thoughts, feelings, hopes and fears. They do not need to be "summoned" up for any reason.

Good Wins in the End Because God Is in Control

Though we will go through some terrible times very soon, good will eventually triumph over evil. Evil must have its "day." It has something to do with the balance that must exist here on earth. Though it may not seem so at all times in today's world, God is always in control.

Jesus Christ will return to the earth and bless the people who loved him and kept his commandments. The obedient will receive tremendous blessings, including His presence, when he reigns once again. It will be a wonderful time, very similar to what it is like in the paradise part of the spirit world. Through some process, the evil spirits will not be able to influence those who remain. This wonderful time of peace and happiness is not very far off, and I believe that many of us now living will make it through the tribulation that lies ahead to experience the joyous times that follow. The Lord will have a remnant of people left to greet Him and help to build up and establish His kingdom. Others who survive will be so sick of death, hate, and war that they will finally be ready to learn God's ways. God our Father wants all of His children to make it back to Him having had a successful journey. Those who do not reject His message of love and helping others will have success.

CHAPTER 7

Commonly Asked Questions and Answers

The following questions and replies are taken from transcripts of several different presentations that Sarah made during the five years before the first publication of this book. The questions are listed as Q1, Q2 etc. Occasionally, there are follow up questions as well. In that case they are listed as Q1a and Q1b.

Q1a: You Say Bad Things That Happen to Us Are Really for Our Good and Almost Nothing Happens by Accident?

Almost everything that happens to us in our lives, every person that we meet, all of it is part of the plan, very little of it is by accident. The circumstances surrounding our lives are all part of a divine plan of which we are a part. What we do when life throws us a curve is up to us, and so the choices we make are very important. We also need to understand that forces are working hard to arrange circumstances for us and then to influence how we respond to them. Do you think that good and evil spirits do not pull strings in our lives to make things happen? They absolutely do. Do you think you could travel down all of the paths throughout your life and by coincidence run into just the right person at just the right time, in just the right place without some help? God sometimes arranges circumstances so that everything that happens to us can work for our benefit, if we allow it to.

The "terrible" experiences of my life have allowed me to help hundreds of people who are going through similar experiences. I do not ever look at any experience in my life as horrible anymore. The Lord does not give us these experiences as punishments, and not even necessarily as trials. Events do occur to us due to natural consequences. The Lord then orchestrates events to help us benefit from them.

Q1b: Are You Saying That God Doesn't Cause Bad Things as A Test for Us? He Did Not Cause Hitler to Kill People?

No, God did not cause those terrible situations to happen. God does not work that way. However, certain tragedies are allowed to involve individuals. Often these can be the natural consequences for bad decisions. Also, there are many hardships that just happen over which we have no control, they just happen.

Before I attempted suicide, I did not believe there was a God or anyone in a heaven that could love me and still allow me to go through the terrible punishments I had to endure. Now I look at it just the other way around. I can now talk to people who are sick, in despair, sorrowful, or who have broken marriages. I have compassion for them in their situation and the words come to me that will lift or elevate these people. I know that if I had not been given those experiences, I would not have the understanding or empathy for them.

Since the beginning of time, individuals have taken their own lives for one reason or another. This is not a new phenomenon. However, in our current time, suicide has become an epidemic among adults and even worse among our youth. People who make this regrettable choice do it under the false assumption or belief that it will solve all their problems. They believe they can just remove themselves from this mortal world with all of its challenges. Some of their anguish may be because of the death of a loved one, the loss of a romantic relationship, feelings of inadequacy in their career, or just life in general.

The problem with this is that you never really leave these painful feelings behind. When you cross over to the other side, you may not suffer from physical pain any longer, but your spirit still keeps the same attitudes, perspectives, and thought patterns you have developed during this life. If you hate others or yourself, and fail to forgive, or if you feel bitterness, regret, or anger, these same feelings remain with you in the world of spirits, except they are now magnified.

You do not automatically change into a different person. There is a process we must work through, and measured steps of progression that take time and effort. It is more difficult for spirits on the other side to overcome bad habits, and unrighteous wants and desires than it is while we are in our physical bodies on earth.

The person that ends their life also has added mental anguish when they discover all the potential and great blessings they forfeited. These are blessings that could have come to them if they had worked through their trials while in mortality.

For a period of time, before publishing the first version of this book, I had helped to counsel a beautiful young girl named Erika. Her parents had sought ecclesiastical and professional help for her, but to no avail. She had attempted suicide on three different occasions. When she first came to me, I could clearly see the pain and desperation in her soul. I recognized and understood what she was feeling and what she needed, because of my own experience.

After a few years of continued encouragement, she completely changed her entire life for the better. She became active in her Church, her family relationships greatly improved, and she received many wonderful blessings that never would have been hers if she had followed through with her original plan to give up.

Our lives are like a huge puzzle. There may be a thousand pieces that we need to put together before we can see the entire picture. We may only have a hundred of those pieces at any given point in our lives. This makes it difficult for us to make a lot of sense without all of the pieces. That is why we have to live in faith. Our Father in Heaven has all of the pieces and He can see what is in store for us from the beginning to the end. This is why we, as His spirit children, need to learn to trust His plan and the potential He knows is possible for us to achieve, despite all the challenges we face.

I look back on some hurtful situations that happened to me shortly before the first publication of this book. I shed plenty of tears and prayed for someone I loved very much, probably more than I have ever in my entire life and yet I knew that there was a purpose for what I went through. I continue to learn from these "unfriendly experiences" and I know that the Savior is in total control, even during the most trying times in my life.

Q2: If There Are No Insects in The Spirit World Why Do We Have Them Here?

They are here because insects give balance to nature. They serve a purpose in the form of plagues. They also serve a purpose in pestering mankind. There is a balance in mortal nature that they do not have or need in the spirit world, as they are not necessary there. Insects also have intelligence, but they are creatures of a lower intelligence, serving a lower purpose.

Q3a: Did You See or Learn Anything In Regards To The Mark of The Beast or The Evil Kingdom Described in The Bible?

I learned a little about the mark of the beast, not because I asked questions directly concerning it, but in order to understand why some of the events that were presently happening, and going to happen on the earth. It was explained to me that there is an evil kingdom here on earth that is directed by Satan. There are people on earth who serve Satan, just like there are people on earth who serve God and Jesus. Some serve Satan knowing who they serve and are pure evil. Others serve him, not understanding exactly who they are serving.

Most of the work of this evil kingdom is done in secret, in darkness, by people who plot together to force everyone in the world to serve them and their master, Satan. There are so many now serving Satan instead of God. It is as if there are armies all over the world working towards this goal. They have been at it for a long time and are getting close to success. Their success will be the time when darkness, chaos, terror and evil will reign supreme for a short period of time.

Q3b: Explain What You Mean by This Satanic Goal of World Conquest?

The whole plan has been plotted out by this secret society of Satan's followers as they have listened to his whisperings. These armies of evil people have plotted towards a one world government and a one world religion for centuries. Their plans include the mark of the beast. This mark will force everyone away from God so that they will want to serve Satan instead. Only a very few people will refuse to do this.

Most people believe that there will be some sort of literal mark of the beast, the implant in the hand or on the forehead. That is true, though I did not see it. In addition to the physical mark, I learned that people are going to come to realize that some of us already have taken the spiritual mark of the beast upon themselves. We live in a modern Babylon and are living as a part of the kingdom of the beast. The mark of the beast in the forehead, in a spiritual sense, is thinking and acting in the ways of Babylon, thinking of the material possessions, the wants, beauty, vanity and pride. The spiritual mark in the hand represents the selfishness and greed as we reach out and take everything that the world has to offer. We are drawn in to these temptations in various ways, both overtly and subtly. It does not mean they need to put a chip in your forehead to fulfill the prophecy. For most of us, the spiritual mark has already come to pass. We take the spiritual mark of the beast when we sign up for more credit cards and go into debt for selfish reasons. We want, we want, we want more. We want the most expensive car. We want a huge house. It is all for personal selfishness. It is all directed at self-gratification. It comes from a self-centered attitude, which is just the opposite of how we should use our means to help others.

People serve Satan's kingdom, or the kingdom of the beast, by acts of intimate relationships outside of marriage. The use of drugs and alcohol supports a culture that promotes prostitution, murder, thievery, lying, rape, and every other evil practice. When women wear revealing clothes, or hardly any clothes at all, this is the same type of fashion that follows the pattern that Satan used to destroy morality since the time of Adam. Sodom and Gomorrah are the best-known examples of this process, but I learned that every time a society has been destroyed, you will find this same revealing style of apparel.

We serve Satan by supporting and having abortions. This is a selfish, devilish-inspired act which destroys the sacred role of motherhood. The very moment the male and female cells come together; you have created a new life. No matter how small this tiny cell is, it is still forming a human being. It is now well known that aborted babies are used for evil purposes. Women who abort these babies out of selfishness are denying this precious being the right to have life. God our Father has told us that, "Thou shalt not kill." This means any living soul, even if it is only the size of the head of a pin. Anyone who kills will suffer the condemnation of hell.

We also serve the adversary by producing and listening to vulgar and violent music or by watching movies with this same kind of content. These are recruiting tools of Satan, and people who listen to and watch them invite dark spirits into their lives and give these spirits power over themselves.

Q4: Do We as Spirits Ever Get to Come Back to Earth After We Die?

Oh, yes. For example, everyone is allowed to come back for his or her own funeral. People can come back for special occasions, like seeing their son or daughter getting married or some other important event. It would be possible to be assigned as a guardian angel or a guiding angel for a relative and so spend a lot of time on earth. However, good people who die are busy with activities in the spirit world and do not have time to waste without purpose.

Often our loved ones who have passed on to the spirit world visit us is in our dreams or when we are in the alpha awareness state. This is when we are more easily susceptible to spiritual influence. They whisper to us and relay information and ideas during this time. Unfortunately, this works for both good and evil spirits. The evil spirits also try to use this sleep state, often causing terrible dreams and nightmares. It isn't just a little child's prayer to ask Heavenly Father to watch over us during the night and to keep our souls safe. It should be part of our prayers every night as well. I learned that there is real power in prayer and God hears every sincere prayer. However, He often answers our prayers in His own due time, and in ways we may not expect.

Q5: Are There Such Things as Ghosts?

Yes. Many call them "ghosts," but they are actually people who have passed away and sometimes remain on earth. Sometimes a person dies and they do not realize it. For a few moments, I did not understand that I had left my body, even as I was looking at it. Occasionally, a person refuses to recognize that their life has ended. They are free to wander as spirits as long as they want to, visiting loved ones and places where they used to live. There are mischievous spirits which can enter a home to frighten the occupants by knocking over furniture, making noises, and opening and closing doors. There is a difference between an evil spirit entering a home and one of these formerly living mischievous spirits. Evil spirits can actually harm a person. People have been pushed, knocked down stairs, and thrown against walls by them.

Q6: Why Do Some People Have So Many Talents While Others Have So Few?

It has to do somewhat with what they learned during their pre-mortal life. A person can also develop new talents if they have the desire to search them out and discover them. Those with great gifts or talents may have tremendous trials and difficulties to overcome, but with perseverance and practice they can create beautiful paintings, inspiring music, great literature, and other notable accomplishments. Many people do not realize that those who have the ability to lift up the downtrodden or comfort those who mourn also have a special gift.

It is usually very easy to pick out very great spirits such as Mother Theresa, Martin Luther King, The Dahlia Lama, Gandhi, Abraham Lincoln, George Washington, and many others. Following Christopher Reeves' injury, when he was completely paralyzed, he remained happy and positive and was a great example of courage to people all over the world. He never felt sorry for himself. In my view, he was a man with a "special gift."

134

Of course, there are also those who use their abilities to lead people to do what is wrong. Some evil men have used the gift of being great orators to enlist others to cause the death of millions of people. These men include Hitler, Stalin, Mao Tse Tung, and others. In our time, there have been men like Hugh Hefner, who contributed to the decline of decency and morality in our country and throughout the world. Unfortunately, there are many very talented actors, actresses and musicians, both male and female, who promote the dark kingdom by their lewd dress and lack of morals. There will be a very heavy price to pay for such ungodly and selfish actions.

Q7: Is There a Way to Avoid the Terrible Things You Saw - The Plagues and Destruction?

Yes. We can easily avoid everything I saw; it is not written in stone. It is actually very simple. Come back to God! Keep God's commandments like we used to do. This country was founded on the principle of serving God and His beloved son Jesus Christ and keeping their commandments, which are outlined in the Bible. As long as the people in this country kept the commandments they were blessed, but when they did not, they suffered the consequences.

I know that the reason these terrible events will be inflicted upon the people in this country and the world is because the majority of them have forsaken God. They are more interested in making money, having fun, and self-indulgence than helping each other. They don't hesitate to hurt or cheat others to get ahead, either. It seems that they do everything they can to forget God and push Him away. When we do that, there will be great devastation. God will withdraw His protection and blessings from the people. This allows Satan and his cohorts to have more power.

Satan and his followers have turned many, and are continuing to lead many people away from God to do Satan's will.

135

They have wanted to take control of the people in the world, and have been planning and working towards that goal from the beginning. They succeeded with the people during Noah's time and they are succeeding with the majority of the people now. I know that a large portion of our society is as wicked now as it was during the time of Noah, and Sodom and Gomorrah just before they were destroyed. If we want to stop the destruction which is coming, then we need to repent and change how we are living our lives, and we need to do it very quickly. When we have God our Father and His son Jesus Christ soundly in our lives, then we have no need to fear. God will protect those who love Him and keep His commandments.

Q8: Did You See Anything About the Rapture?

What most people think of the rapture is actually the time when Christ comes down from heaven to take those who have followed him back with him. It will happen after the time of chaos and tribulation, but just before the final, complete destruction of the wicked by the huge ball of fire. The people, who were in the cities of light were the very people who would be taken up during the rapture. They were the people who continued to keep the commandments of God, who still worshiped Jesus and wouldn't deny Him. They were those who practiced charity. The Holy Spirit protected them and guided them to gather to the cities of light for protection during the period of tribulation. Those good people were on the earth for most of the chaos and destruction, though they did not suffer to the same extent the wicked did. I knew that God was protecting them from most of the devastation, but what they had to endure was still very difficult.

Q9: How Soon Do You Think These Events Will Happen and How Long Have You Talked About the Buildings Falling in New York City?

I have been talking about the buildings falling down in New York City since 1979, ever since I felt I needed to tell my story to more people. In 1999, Channel 13 News interviewed me for four hours on my experience.

People have asked me how soon I think the next major events will occur. I believe they are coming very soon. When I saw the towers fall on September 11th, 2001, I knew that was part of what I had seen in my experience. The fall of the Twin Towers was a sign of the events that would continue to occur in our country. This event will be followed by hard economic times and continuing terrorist attacks.

We can see that the country is in a recession now, headed for hyperinflation, followed by a depression. In other words, we are facing hard economic times. If people have not physically prepared for this by being out of debt, storing food and water, and most importantly, being spiritually prepared, then they will suffer.

Q10: Are Some Places Safer Than Other Places?

As far as places or states that are generally safer than others, there really aren't any. All of America, and other countries around the world, are going to be affected by what is coming. I believe North America will be affected the most. I would not want to live anywhere near any coastal areas, and I would not live anywhere near a volcano. New eruptions will appear where none have been in the past.

I saw major devastations take place in New York City, Los Angeles, San Francisco, and Salt Lake City. However, almost every city will be hit with some devastation. The center of the United States, somewhere near Kansas City and St. Louis was hit particularly hard with a nuclear bomb and a tremendous earthquake. This quake caused all of the land along the Mississippi River from the Great Lakes to the Gulf of Mexico to sink, and that space was all under water. The Great Lakes became a continuous sea and the United States was split in two. When this huge mega-quake occurs in the middle of the country, San Francisco will completely turn upside-down. At this time the entire earth will be in commotion.

Common sense should tell us that when the electricity gets shut down by an attack on the grid, it would be terrible to be in any big city. For many years I felt that if times got bad, I would love to have a little house out in the country, a place where I could have a little garden and be away from the mainstream. I lived in large cities for many years, but I was finally able to move to a much smaller town. Eventually, even the small towns will be affected. The only safe places were the cities of light that were scattered across the country. When the crises begin, if you are close enough to the Lord, He will direct you to one of these gathering places of light.

Q11: How Can We Prepare for What Is Coming?

A time will come, and could last perhaps three or four years, when there will not be any food, water or electricity. During part of that time, it will be so dark due to earthquake and volcanic activity, that it will be nearly impossible to grow food in a garden.

Over the years I have run into many people, some religious and some not, who have felt very strongly about storing food. Other necessities also include winter clothing, medical needs, and other survival equipment, in case of a long-term emergency.

Y2K started people thinking for the first time about all the problems that we would face if the electricity was shut down for a long period of time. With the attacks on the towers on

September 11th, people began to realize that anything could happen at any time without warning. The time will come when the trucks and railroads that deliver goods will not be running. The resulting unrest and rioting will seriously derail our society as we know it.

I would advise people to also have the means to protect themselves and their families against the marauding gangs that will be killing people for their food and possessions. It would be wise to have like-minded friends who have also prepared themselves so that we can gather together to help protect each other. There is safety in numbers.

I must add something else very important. The best preparation we can make is not with food, water and other material necessities. These are definitely very important, but the most important preparation is spiritual preparation. Keeping the Ten Commandments is very important. Not enough people in America or in the world do that anymore, and I believe that is part of the reason why evil is becoming so strong and why evil will have its day.

It is important to know that there will be a special protection given to those people who faithfully keep the Sabbath day holy. It is a day for worshiping God and serving others, and not for sports, entertainment or work.

Being kind to others, forgiving those who have harmed you, reading the scriptures, visiting the sick, and praying are also very important in our spiritual preparation. I can promise you that it won't matter if you have tons of food and a whole army with you. If we are not listening to what the Lord has asked of us, we will not have the protection He has promised if we had been listening to His warnings. Leviticus 26:2-12 contains the blessings pertaining to Sabbath Worship.

Q12: Did You Ever Find Out Who the Beautiful Woman Was That You Saw?

A few years after my NDE, my sisters and I were packing up my mother's belongings because we were forced to put her in an assisted living facility. None of us were able to care for her any more. While cleaning out her basement, I came across a large photograph album. Looking through it page by page, I saw the picture of the woman who sent me back from the Spirit World. I asked my sister who this woman was. She replied, "It is our mother's mother, Sarah," who died shortly after I was born.

Grandmother Sarah

My birth name was LaNelle, but since that day I began to use Sarah as my name. It makes me feel more like there is a closer connection between the two of us.

Q13: Will We Look the Same in The Spirit World as We Do Here?

We will be able to recognize our loved ones and friends. However, our spirits are much more beautiful than our physical bodies. Here are no weight concerns, no deformities, no scars, no physical defects, and no imperfections. There is a false conception that angels have wings. Spirit beings who serve as angels travel instantly through a conduit of light and energy. The concept of angels as winged beings began in the Christian era with Tertullian in 160 A.D.

Q14: Why Do You Think You Had This Experience?

To tell you the truth, I am not sure why. I don't think of myself as someone special, actually just the opposite. I think of myself as very ordinary.

My experience changed me and turned my life around, especially concerning the hate and anger I had for my father. That hate was consuming and destroying me. For twelve years or so after my NDE, I thought that this experience was just for me. I shared it with a few people, but it was almost always one person at a time.

When I had heart and kidney failure in 1994, I nearly crossed over again. Since then, I have felt a strong need to share my experience with many others. I started sharing my story with large groups of people, but even after that, I felt it was not enough. Eventually I was approached by two publishers who wanted to make my story into a book. I believe the reason I remember almost everything that happened is so that I will be able to share it all with the world and perhaps help someone.

I am not a prophetess or a psychic. I am just a simple person who had a remarkable experience. I did not believe in God when my visit to the Spirit World happened. I didn't even believe there was a God. Now I know He lives.

Without exception, when I share my experience, people tell me afterward that I have answered important questions they have been struggling with, or helped change their life in a positive direction. I am beginning to understand that this is perhaps the reason I died and came back. My hope is that I can help more people to draw closer to our Father in Heaven and Jesus Christ, and help them to have a better understanding of the purpose of life.

About The Author

Sarah is a unique and remarkable person. Those who have come to know her have quickly learned to love her. Since first publicly telling this story, monetary gain from the effort has never been a motivating factor. She lives in a small, rented apartment on a very limited income but she is exceptionally generous. Because of her blindness, she doesn't own a car and needs someone to accompany her whenever she leaves her house. However, she feels that she has sufficient for her needs.

Sarah (LaNelle) Age 29, 1979

As you read about Sarah's experience it will become obvious that her life has not been easy. She is able to hide her pain and fatigue with a quick smile and immediate love and acceptance, even while constantly counseling and inspiring those who have gone through, or are going through tremendous trials of their own. She offers hope, compassion and insight as she is so well qualified and determined to do.

Those who have worked on the book with her wish to express their great satisfaction in the labor to bring this remarkable and very personal experience to you. It has greatly and positively affected us. Our hope is that it will do the same for you as you read and ponder this book. What is written is from Sarah.